STEAM LOCOMOTIVE
Driver's Manual

COVER PHOTO: A steam locomotive crew in perfect harmony – driver with his eyess on the road ahead, fireman feeding the fire. Once it was an environment beyond the reach of the average enthusiast, but no longer, as this book reveals. *(Alan Crotty).*

First published in April 2015

A catalogue record for this book is available from the British Library.

ISBN 978 1 84425 942 7

Library of Congress control no. 2014953500

Published by Haynes Publishing,
Sparkford, Yeovil,
Somerset BA22 7JJ, UK.
Tel: 01963 442030 Fax: 01963 440001
Int. tel: +44 1963 442030
Int. fax: +44 1963 440001
E-mail: sales@haynes.co.uk
Website: www.haynes.co.uk

Haynes North America Inc.,
861 Lawrence Drive, Newbury Park,
California 91320, USA.

Printed in the USA by Odcombe Press LP,
1299 Bridgestone Parkway, La Vergne,
TN 37086.

Acknowledgements

The author wishes to thank everyone who has offered their time and knowledge to aid the production of this book, including those who have contributed photographs.

He would particularly like to thank his fellow volunteers and staff on the Welshpool & Llanfair Light Railway for putting up particularly with his roving camera and constant enquiries. Specific thanks are due to Frank Podmore, John Clark, Roger Pattie, Simon Bowden, Keith Armes and Phil Ellis.

Unless stated otherwise, all photographs are by the author.

Last, but by no means the least, the author must thank his wife Rosemary and children James, Stewart and Megan for tolerating the chaos at home that inevitably resulted from producing this work.

STEAM LOCOMOTIVE
Driver's Manual

The step-by-step guide to preparing, firing
and driving a steam locomotive

Andrew Charman

Contents

OPPOSITE **The view from the cab, here on the Isle of Man Railway, heading into a station with another train waiting.**

ABOVE RIGHT **This book describes the complete procedure for firing and driving a locomotive, from first lighting it up in the morning. Here, Kerr Stuart 0-4-2ST** *Joan* **comes to life in the Llanfair shed.**

Introduction

There are those who believe the age of the steam locomotive ended in 1968, when the last engines were withdrawn from service on the UK's mainlines, as British Railways moved into a future of diesel and electric traction.

In fact, nothing could be further from the truth and even as fires were dropped for the final time in mainline sheds and the locomotives were hauled to scrapyards, the preservation movement was in full swing. The first preserved line, the narrow gauge Talyllyn Railway in Mid-Wales, had by 1968, been running for 17 years in the hands of enthusiasts. Meanwhile, the first standard-gauge passenger line to be preserved, the Bluebell Railway in East Sussex, was approaching the end of its first decade of volunteer operation by that year.

The preservation scene has continued to grow remorselessly ever since to the point where today, more than 45 years after the official 'end of steam', one cannot travel very far in the British Isles without encountering a steam locomotive. Annual guides to the UK's heritage railways lists more than 100 preserved railways and new steam lines created on former BR routes, before one counts the steam centres which feature locomotives in action on many a weekend.

Similarly, interest in miniature railways has never been higher, with new lines springing up alongside standard-gauge heritage railways and in garden centres around the country. While the locomotives on these lines may seem insignificant compared with say a Pacific express loco powering along with a mainline steam special, they are built, and handled, in exactly the same way as their full-size counterparts. This is true right down to the live steam models built by the many model engineering clubs throughout the UK. For those wanting to experience the unique attraction of steam haulage, there is no shortage of opportunity.

BELOW It is more than 40 years since steam locomotives were withdrawn from regular mainline use, but today the fascination with them is stronger than ever. Witness the crowds watching this LMS 'Crab' 2-6-0 arrive at Ramsbottom on the East Lancashire Railway.
(Eddie Bellass)

LEFT The narrow-gauge Talyllyn Railway in mid-Wales started the preservation scene in 1951, and more than half a century on is still going strong. Fletcher Jennings 0-4-2ST *Talyllyn*, built way back in 1864, simmers at Abergynolwyn station.

BELOW Interest in miniature lines has never been stronger, though this one, the Fairbourne Railway in mid-Wales, has been running more than half a century. Miniature engines are handled in exactly the same manner as their full-size counterparts.

RIGHT Scenes like this, at Dallam shed, Warrington, in the 1960s, might have gone for ever…
(Eddie Bellass)

BELOW …but steam locomotives are today being cared for in somewhat more up-to-date conditions – this is the workshops of the Princess Royal Locomotive Trust at Butterley, Derbyshire.

It is easy to ride behind a steam locomotive, you simply buy a ticket. But surely climbing onto the footplate and taking the controls, that is another world only accessed by a hallowed few? Not a bit of it – anyone with a modicum of sense can soon find themselves at the controls of a steam locomotive, in two main ways – either by spending some money, or giving up some time.

The spending money option is the fastest

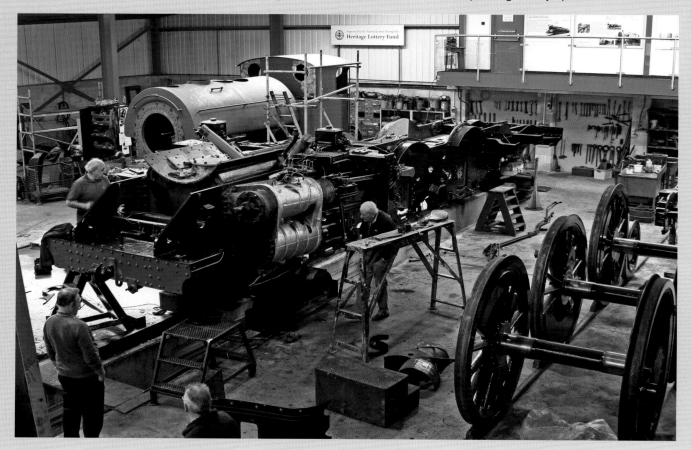

way to the driver's seat. The 'Footplate Experience' or 'Driver Experience' has grown in popularity in recent years, and for many heritage railways now provides an important income stream. On the line where I volunteer, the narrow-gauge Welshpool & Llanfair Light Railway in Wales, our driver-experience days are always sold out before the start of the season.

These days there is a plentiful selection of footplate experiences to choose from, at a wide variety of railways – miniature, narrow and standard gauge – and a wide range of prices. The experiences also vary in their format, so it is wise to do some research to ensure you find a day out that most suits you – especially considering that even for the cheapest experience, you will be spending a significant amount of money. This is likely to be from a couple of hundred pounds upwards.

As an example, the stock Welshpool & Llanfair experience, costing around £400 in 2014, is a half-day course for one person, during which they will drive most of a return trip on the eight-mile line, including the notorious Golfa Bank that climbs at 1 in 29 for almost two miles. This is not just carried out on a

ABOVE For anyone wanting to get on the footplate, volunteering in the workshops at your local preserved railway will be both enjoyable and informative. Here volunteers are seen at work on the Welshpool & Llanfair Light Railway in mid-Wales.

LEFT Never a professional railwayman, the author has learnt much about the mysteries of the steam locomotive from the workshops of the Welshpool & Llanfair Light Railway in mid-Wales. Here he is seen preparing a boiler for inspection.

LEFT The enginemen of the old mainline days were regarded with an air of mystery...
(Eddie Bellass)

locomotive as a train is attached for the entire journey allowing the lucky candidate's family or friends to travel and watch them in action.

In contrast, the standard-gauge Severn Valley Railway, one of the UK's best-known steam lines, offers a range of courses from firing a locomotive with a single coach behind, to driving a loco at the head of a 200-ton train over the entire 32-mile route. Here, prices range from around £300 to £800.

As a total contrast, the 12¼in-gauge Fairbourne Railway includes evening courses in its driver experience programme, for around £100. The standard-gauge Kent & East Sussex Railway offers a 'Footplate Taster' in which the participant rides with the driver and fireman on a return trip, but does not actually do any work – this is a good way to observe what is involved and to decide whether you would enjoy it.

A recent trend providing an inexpensive way of discovering if you might like the idea of spending money on a full footplate experience, is 'Driver for a Fiver'. Run by some railways, usually at special events, it consists of having an extra locomotive in steam on a siding at one of the main stations, where any member of the public can pay just £5 to 'drive' to the end of the siding and back under the close supervision of a qualified driver. It only takes a few minutes, but gives a brief taster of what life is like on the footplate, and could end up changing your life...

In short, most heritage railways offer footplate experiences of some type, and with a little preparation (including reading this book!), one can have a highly enjoyable and informative day out.

LEFT ...and while some have been able to impart their knowledge to today's preserved railway world, it has never been easier to become part of today's generation of locomotive crew.
(Eddie Bellass)

Taking the big step

The next step is to go beyond the day out, to decide that you really would like to fire or drive full-size steam engines on a regular basis. To achieve this will take time. First, simply because there is a lot to learn and secondly, to get the most out of this vocation, you will need it to become a significant hobby.

The vast majority of steam locomotives operating today are run by heritage railways, and while many of them have a core of permanent staff, they are supported by vast numbers of volunteers who spend their spare time manning the railway. This can be a couple of weeks' holiday each year, or on most weekends, quite simply because they enjoy 'playing trains', albeit to a fully professional standard. This is as true of the footplate department as it is the guards, signalmen, station staff, the permanent way crews etc.

Your first step will be to find a heritage railway you like – there are links to listings of heritage lines at the back of this book – then to join the supporting society or company, and to sign up to volunteer on the line. This need not be in the footplate department – you could be in the workshops, helping on the station, tending the gardens, or possibly bringing whatever skills you use in your paid employment to the benefit of the railway.

By volunteering you will be working with other like-minded people, and you will soon discover whether you get on with them and the line in question is for you – it is essential you discover this before committing yourself to the long-term programme that is footplate training. It is also important that you do not just join a railway to drive engines – the most successful and popular volunteers are those whose footplate career is just part of the time they give to the railway.

Different railways have different methods of footplate training – some still follow the way that it was done in British Railways days in the 1960s and before, others have more modern, streamlined programmes. Once you have settled on a railway you like and have become involved, you will soon find your way to getting onto the footplate training roster. When you do, a basic knowledge of how the steam locomotive works will help you immensely – and we will look at that shortly. But first, a little history.

ABOVE Sunny day, hot fire, and a cup of tea on the footplate – what could be better? *(Jon Bowers)*

FOOD ON THE FOOTPLATE

The fried breakfast cooked on the fireman's shovel is the stuff of railway legend, but also something that actually happens on a regular basis. Curiously, it tends to be the most frequent question asked by those taking part in footplate experiences!

The cooking is usually done on the fireman's shovel, after it has been given a good clean of course. It is held over the fire and tilted back slightly, thus forming a 'pan' in which to fry the food. Using cooking oil the traditional breakfast of bacon, sausage and egg can all be cooked, separately or together.

However, these are by no means the only foods that can be footplate fare. The 'warming plate' directly above the firehole door and normally used for keeping oil cans warm, is great for heating pasties or pies, which have first been wrapped in foil, with a covering of newspaper and then a polythene bag. The bag keeps any footplate oil and dirt from the food and if the heat of the fire should melt the bag the newspaper offers an extra layer of protection. Tins of food can also be warmed in a similar manner, but make sure a hole is pierced in the top first.

During a gala event on the author's railway, a loco crew knew they would have a long lay-over at the far terminus, so before the outward trip they placed jacket potatoes wrapped in foil in the locomotive's smokebox. At the other end of the journey they had cooked to the perfect degree for a leisurely lunch. It can be guaranteed that whatever food one chooses, it will taste so much better once cooked on the footplate.

Chapter One

A brief steam locomotive history

Many and complex works have been written concerning the long and glorious history of the steam locomotive. Looking back is not what this book is about, but some basic information, outlining how the machine we wish to drive today came about, may be useful. This is because many of the basic elements of the steam engine were created in the earliest days of railways, and have remained little changed ever since.

OPPOSITE Sir Nigel Gresley's streamlined A4 class, built for the London & North Eastern Railway, were in many ways, a culmination in steam locomotive design. One of them, *Mallard,* set the still-standing world speed record for steam traction in 1938. This is preserved example No 60009 *Union of South Africa*, on a mainline special in 1988. *(Eddie Bellass)*

The first steam engines, which evolved in the late 18th century, were enormous stationary units built mainly for pumping water from colliery workings and the like. A popular myth claims that the steam engine was invented by James Watt whereas in fact, he improved the stationary engines of Thomas Newcomen, making them capable of powering a wheel. However, Watt never constructed a locomotive, although one of his employees did build a working model of a steam-powered road carriage.

In 1804, Cornish engineer Richard Trevithick built the first steam railway locomotive, which, on 21 February that year, was recorded as hauling the first train along the waggonway rails of the Penydarren iron works near Merthyr Tydfil in South Wales.

Trevithick later demonstrated a locomotive on a circular track in London, close to today's Euston station, but could not make his engines light enough to avoid breaking the cast-iron, right-angled plateway rails then in use in industry. It was thought locos needed to be heavy to provide enough adhesion to move trains.

Matthew Murray built a twin-cylinder locomotive, the *Salamanca* in 1812 for the Middleton Colliery in Leeds. This used a cog wheel on a rack built into the side of the track, thus providing adhesion and negating the need for the loco to be heavy.

A year later came *Puffing Billy* built by William Hedley and Christopher Blackett for the Wylam Colliery railway in Northumberland. By using eight wheels on four axles the loco reduced the weight on each, making it the first successful steam locomotive relying on adhesion only. *Puffing Billy* was later modified to use six wheels and finally four, in which condition it can today be seen on display in London's Science Museum as the oldest surviving steam locomotive.

Enter the scene, the most famous name in early railway history – George Stephenson. In 1814 he built a locomotive, the *Blucher* for Killingworth Colliery, also in Northumberland. This engine used wheels with flanges on their inside, rendering the fragile plateway rails redundant, and effectively setting a blueprint for future railway construction. By 1825 Stephenson had built *Locomotion* to run on the world's first public railway, the Stockton & Darlington Railway.

OPPOSITE *Catch Me Who Can* was railway pioneer Richard Trevithick's third locomotive. Built in 1808 it was demonstrated on a circular track in London. In 2010, this replica was nearing completion at the Severn Valley Railway in Shropshire.

BELOW *Locomotion* is widely regarded as the first truly successful steam locomotive and was built in 1825 for the Stockton & Darlington Railway by George Stephenson. The original is now preserved at Darlington North Road station, while this is a working replica built in 1975 and normally resident at Beamish Museum in County Durham.

RIGHT *Rocket*, built in 1829 by George Stephenson and winner of the Rainhill locomotive trials, is one of the best-known steam locomotives in the world. The original is now displayed in London's Science Museum. This is one of at least three replicas built of the engine, but the only working example.

The famous Rainhill Trials followed in 1829 to establish the best type of steam locomotive to work the planned Liverpool & Manchester Railway, which would be the first to connect cities and be primarily built to carry passengers. As is well known, Stephenson won the trials with his *Rocket*, a locomotive with cylinders that acted directly on to the driving wheels and

having many features that would remain part of basic locomotive design for centuries.

The success of the Liverpool & Manchester Railway, particularly in terms of passenger traffic, set off the age of railway mania as new lines spread across the country. By the 1850s, rails had reached London though the lines were not permitted to run into the city centre, thus

RIGHT An early locomotive on the Liverpool & Manchester Railway was Stephenson's *Planet*. This was the first engine to use inside-mounted cylinders. This replica works today at the Museum of Science & Industry, which is at the Liverpool & Manchester Railway's old Liverpool Road terminus in Manchester.
(Eddie Bellass)

LEFT The Stirling Single, built in 1870 for the Great Northern Railway and today displayed at the National Railway Museum, is a good example of a 19th century passenger locomotive with large, single driving wheels.

producing the ring of terminal stations we still have today. The pioneers solved the problem by heading below the surface. The Metropolitan, opened in 1863, and running initially from the Great Western Railway's Paddington station and was the world's first underground railway, although not, as is sometimes claimed, the first 'tube line'. It was built by the cut-and-cover method of digging a trench in the surface, inserting the railway and covering it over to form underground tunnels. The first true tube line was the City & South London Railway opened in 1890 and today part of the Northern Line.

The railway age also quickly spread across the world, especially in India, then under British rule, which adopted an extensive railway system at a very early stage. While Continental builders were to play their own major role in the history of railways, British manufacturers exported their railway technology to the world throughout the steam age, much of which remains in use today in places such as South Africa and India.

Stephenson and his son Robert were at the forefront of railway expansion, and the 4ft 8½in gauge (1,435mm) to which they had built the Liverpool & Manchester Railway became the standard.

Locomotive technology moved forward apace too, with two distinct types of engine appearing: those with large, often single, driving wheels designed for hauling passenger trains at speed, and those with smaller driving wheels coupled together, offering greater pulling power for hauling heavy goods trains at slower speed.

As railways became more popular, further engineers came onto the scene with their own interpretations of steam locomotives, some very good, some quite eccentric. The Crampton was a prime example of the latter – some of

LEFT The enormous single driving wheel and unusual outside eccentric gearing of the Crampton loco, a type little used in the UK but widely adopted on the Continent. This engine was photographed in the French National Railway Museum in Mulhouse.
(Gareth Houghton)

ABOVE Although no original Great Western Railway broad gauge locomotives survived, other than the South Devon Railway's 'coffeepot' *Tiny*, now preserved at Buckfastleigh, two new-build replicas have been produced. Both are now at the Didcot Railway Centre, this being the National Collection's 4-2-2 *Iron Duke*. The other is 2-2-2 *Fire Fly*.
(Peter Nicholson)

these had huge driving wheels, of 8ft or more in diameter, mounted behind the firebox, thus allowing the use of a large, low boiler. Crampton designs were characterised by large heating surfaces and big steam pipes, and while they found little favour in Britain they were much more popular in France and Germany.

Thomas Crampton's early years were spent with the Great Western Railway working for the noted engineer Marc Brunel, most famous for the building of the first tunnel under the River Thames in London. However, Brunel would soon be eclipsed by his own son, who in terms of steam locomotive development was as eccentric as Crampton, but ended up far better known.

Success in many engineering projects saw Isambard Kingdom Brunel appointed chief engineer to the Great Western Railway. He turned his back on Stephenson's 'standard gauge' and chose a 7ft 0¼in (2,140mm) broad gauge. He designed his own locomotives to this gauge, but they were not greatly successful until the appointment of 20-year-old Daniel Gooch as the GWR locomotive superintendent,

who greatly improved these designs as well as producing his own.

Together with Brunel, Gooch established the GWR locomotive and carriage works at Swindon in 1842, a town which was to become one of the focal points of the steam industry.

The GWR would later produce other major figures in steam locomotive development, not least George Jackson Churchward who, as chief mechanical engineer between 1902 and 1922, introduced many technical advances that we will discuss later in this book. Notably, these included standardised designs, the flat-top firebox and the tapered boiler. These were usually superheated and to high pressure. Some of these innovations were of his own design, others the result of studying locomotive practice on the Continent.

Churchward retired in 1922 but died in ironic circumstances 11 years later when, while inspecting a rotten sleeper on the GWR mainline at Swindon, he was hit by a train hauled by a 'Castle' class locomotive. This was designed by his direct successor, Charles

Benjamin Collett, and heavily influenced by Churchward's engines.

Even William Stanier, who as CME of the London, Midland & Scottish Railway, would produce one of the most successful steam locomotives of UK history, the 4-6-0 'Black Five' class, was born in Swindon and spent his early career employed by the Great Western. He was headhunted by the LMS in 1931 and his Class 5 mixed-traffic design, first produced in 1934, was a direct precursor to the standardised classes introduced by British Railways after the Second World War.

Returning to Brunel's broad gauge, while it offered some advantages, the trains being roomy, more stable and therefore capable of high speeds, it was out of step with the rest of the country. Following Brunel's death in 1859 the GWR was progressively converted to standard gauge, the last broad-gauge rails taken up in 1892.

The late 19th century also saw many advances on the narrow-gauge railways, arising from the tracks of around 2ft (600mm) gauge as used in industry, particularly in collieries and mines. Trains on these lines were initially horse-drawn, but they were soon replaced by small steam locomotives and the narrow gauge played its often forgotten part in locomotive development, particularly on the seemingly insignificant 2ft-gauge Festiniog (today Ffestiniog) Railway in North Wales.

This line produced many firsts, including bogie coaches on a UK railway, but became most famous for proving the practicality of the articulated locomotives of Scottish engineer Robert Francis Fairlie. Some of these, the double-Fairlie-type, look just like two locos placed back-to-back, consisting of one, long, double-ended boiler with a central firebox and cab, and a pair of power bogies fed by flexible steam pipes.

The first successful version, the *Little Wonder* ran on the Ffestiniog in 1869 and was able to haul heavy loads around tight curves on this narrow gauge, and while not generally adopted in the UK, some Fairlie engines found favour abroad, particularly in British colonies. The Fairlie's bogie arrangement also predicted the layout of diesel and electric locomotives almost a century later.

Another articulated locomotive type invented, but little used, in Britain found great success

BELOW The Festiniog (today Ffestiniog) Railway was the standard-bearer for the expansion of the narrow gauge across the world, particularly in locomotive development. The England 0-4-0STs (centre) were among the earliest steam locomotives on the narrow gauge, the single and double-Fairlies (left and right) being some of the most powerful, relative to their size.

RIGHT The Garratt articulated engine was a prime example of UK locomotive technology exported across the globe. This 2ft-gauge example was the first built, for use in Tasmania. Preserved by the Ffestiniog Railway it was restored to work on the revived Welsh Highland Railway. *(Courtesy Ffestiniog Railway)*

RIGHT The Meyer was another development of the articulated principle much used on the Continent. However, this Kitson-Meyer, *Monarch,* worked at Bowaters paper mill in Kent and was the last narrow-gauge steam locomotive built for industrial use in the UK.

abroad, particularly in Africa. This was the Garratt, created by Herbert William Garratt and built initially by Beyer, Peacock of Manchester. It had forward and rear tenders with power bogies underneath and the boiler slung between them on a cradle, producing great power. The first example was constructed in 1909 for a railway in Tasmania and can still be seen today at the Ffestiniog/Welsh Highland Railway in North Wales.

Around the globe engineers produced various ideas for articulated locomotives, such as the Meyer and Mallet, and the curious Shays, Climaxes and Heislers which used a profusion of gears. They were powerful but slow, and were used particularly on logging lines in America and Australia.

Generally however, the design of the steam locomotive would follow the same basic principles until the middle of the 20th century when it began to be replaced, at least in the UK, by diesel and electric locomotives. The

later steam locomotives simply got bigger and more powerful, culminating in such classics as the London & North Eastern Railway Pacifics built by Sir Nigel Gresley in the 1920s, one of which, A4 class *Mallard* set a world speed record for steam traction in 1938 of 125.88mph (202.58 km/h) on the East Coast Main Line near Grantham, Lincolnshire.

Britain's four big railway companies were nationalised from 1 January 1948, becoming one organisation, British Railways. The new management created a range of standard designs of steam locomotive directly influenced by those of the likes of Collett and Stanier. But now, as far as Britain's mainline railways were concerned, the steam locomotive was in the twilight of its career.

Modernisation saw the spread of diesel and electric locomotives and multiple units, and the rundown of the steam locomotive fleet. During this period the locos were increasingly neglected and were allowed to work trains in

ABOVE Perhaps among the most unusual locomotives of all were the Shays, used widely in America on logging lines, where their slow speed was advantageous. The cylinders were mounted vertically, halfway along the boiler, driving through a series of gears. *(Mike Bickford)*

OPPOSITE The Stanier 'Black Five' 4-6-0s, designed originally for the London Midland & Scottish Railway, were among the most successful steam locomotives built. Some 18 have been preserved. This is No 44806 when at the Llangollen Railway.

ABOVE The Stanier 'Black Fives' were equally adept at hauling heavy freight or passenger trains. No 44821 is seen on a Llandudno working in the 1960s. *(Eddie Bellass)*

BELOW The post-war period saw nationalisation followed by the introduction of standard designs by BR, such as the 'Britannia' class No 70031 *Byron* pictured here. But the period also saw the rise of diesel and electric locomotives. *(Eddie Bellass)*

RIGHT The final days of steam on Britain's mainlines were characterised by filthy, neglected locomotives. This is Dallam shed, Warrington in the 1960s. *(Eddie Bellass)*

BELOW The final class of locomotives built for British Railways, the 9F 2-10-0 heavy haulers, had only around 10 years' work before being withdrawn. This is one of nine in preservation, No 92214, seen on the East Lancashire Railway. *(Eddie Bellass)*

filthy conditions – so much so that enthusiasts resorted to after-dark twilight raids into motive power depots merely to clean the engines.

In 1968 it was all over – the last standard-gauge timetabled steam workings ran on British Railways and hundreds of locomotives were committed to scrap yards, some almost new. The last locomotive built for British Railways, 9F class No 92220 *Evening Star*, was withdrawn in March 1965 and so had just five years' work before being retired, thankfully to be preserved.

Equally thankfully, preservation beckoned for far more locomotives than the enthusiasts watching the last special trains of 1968 could ever have dreamed of. As stated in the Introduction, by the time BR abandoned steam, the preservation movement was well underway with heritage lines being opened across the country. Over the following decades the scene mushroomed to the healthy industry it has become today.

Perhaps there is no better demonstration of this than Barry scrapyard in South Wales. Beginning in 1957, the Woodham brothers bought almost 300 withdrawn locomotives from British Railways, but they were scrapmen with

hearts, or perhaps an eye for business. Over the next 33 years they concentrated on cutting up redundant wagons before tackling the more complex steam engines.

Woodham's yard became a mecca for enthusiasts as various preservation groups raised funds to buy locomotives, along with some wealthy individuals. The last engine to leave Barry, in 1990, followed a remarkable 212 others into preservation.

Away from UK shores, however, the rundown of steam in some countries was not quite so rapid. For many years, enthusiasts prepared to travel could enjoy steam performing a proper job of work, particularly in South Africa, the Far East and the Soviet Union, with the falling back of the Iron Curtain opening up new possibilities for the more adventurous steam fan. While such venues have declined in number, there are still places, China for example, where one can see steam at work today.

One does not have to travel overseas these days, however. Within a few years of the end of steam in 1968, British Rail's ban on steam running on mainlines was lifted, leading to

BELOW Lines of withdrawn locomotives became a familiar sight during the last days of steam on British Railways. However, many survived the scrapyard to be saved for preservation and returned to service. It is difficult to imagine the sad sights of the scrapyards today, but locomotives awaiting restoration, such as here in 2010 on the Mid-Hants Railway, can give some idea of what the scenes were like.

ABOVE Even before steam disappeared from the mainlines, enthusiasts were beginning to save branch and narrow-gauge lines. First of all was the Talyllyn in Wales, seen here on its reopening in 1951. *(Courtesy Talyllyn Railway Archive)*

BELOW From small beginnings the railway preservation movement has grown to become a major part of today's tourist industry. This is Kidderminster station on the Severn Valley Railway, which provides 19th century ambience for a 21st century audience.

growing numbers of steam charters, which today, have become major businesses with steam-hauled specials running on the UK network most weeks of the year.

The private railway business, meanwhile, is an even bigger success story, the savage railway cutbacks of Dr Beeching in the 1960s producing many abandoned branch lines and secondary routes ripe for takeover by enthusiasts who basically wanted to 'play trains'. These have become solid tourist attractions and now, in the 21st century, with the advantages of rail travel over road once more in the spotlight, many of these lines are again being seen as viable transport links, with heritage steam at weekends and the potential to be supplemented by commuter traffic on weekdays.

Perhaps indicative of the new breed is the narrow gauge Welsh Highland Railway running through the middle of Snowdonia. The original line, fully opened in 1923, was never a commercial success and was closed by the start of the Second World War. Reopened in stages by the neighbouring Ffestiniog Railway since 1997 using Garratt locomotives and track repatriated from South Africa, the 20-mile line is now seen as a major transport provider removing many cars from the heart of the national park.

The steam locomotive itself has enjoyed a major revival, not only in terms of old engines restored, but completely new engines built. The launch of the new-build A1 Pacific locomotive *Tornado* in 2009 produced front-page headlines around the globe, and not just in the railway press. In addition, totally new narrow-gauge locomotives have been coming out of workshops for some years.

Today, more and more ordinary people are driving steam locomotives. As mentioned in the introduction, 'Driver Experience' days, which see members of the public often paying hundreds of pounds to take the controls of a steam locomotive under expert supervision, are run by many heritage railways, and are usually sold out months in advance.

Many of today's children, growing up almost

ABOVE In November 2010, crowds turned out to watch the first passenger train cross the road in Porthmadog, North Wales, marking the completion of the revived Welsh Highland Railway, a prime example of the success of railway preservation. Both locomotives are replicas of vanished classes, built by new generations of steam enthusiasts. *(Michael Chapman)*

LEFT Perhaps now vying for No. 4472 *Flying Scotsman*'s claim of being 'Britain's most famous loco' is the new-build Peppercorn-designed A1 class 4-6-2 No. 60163 *Tornado.* *(Peter Nicholson)*

ABOVE The hobby of model engineering has seen significant growth in recent years, modellers recreating full-size steam locomotives in miniature, complete in every detail as seen here, working in exactly the same way.

half a century after the end of steam as a regular sight on the national network, are still fascinated far more by steam engines than their diesel and electric successors. Part of this is certainly due to the writings of authors such as the Rev. Awdry and his *Thomas the Tank Engine* books, which, since being turned into TV programmes from the 1980s, has become a worldwide phenomenon. But another reason is possibly because the steam locomotive appears to be a much more alive machine than any diesel or electric engine, a fact that attracts children aged from eight to 80.

They now have plenty of opportunities to see such locos, even on a trip to the garden centre, or the local park. Miniature railways are almost as old as full-size lines, and having gone through a period of decline roughly paralleling

that of full-size steam, have seen a major revival over the past couple of decades. Many a miniature railway, of 15-inch gauge or less, has been opened particularly in garden centres and parks. Steam engines, built by a new breed of specialist manufacturer, have been an essential element of these new lines.

The hobby of model engineering is back on the up again, having seemingly withstood the era of computer games, as more clubs report an upsurge in young members joining up and learning how to construct and operate model locomotives. Even in the garden, steam now rules, with one of the biggest growth areas of the model railway hobby being in outdoor lines of 32/45mm gauge track populated by gas-fired live-steam locomotives.

Yet while the appeal of the steam locomotive has reached out to more people than ever before, how it actually works, and how one makes it work, remains a mystery to many. We'll seek to unravel that mystery in the following pages.

RIGHT The locoman's environment, except this is not quite what it seems. It is actually a 7¼in-gauge model built by Chris Vine, complete in every detail and operated in exactly the same way as its full-size counterpart.

Chapter Two

How a steam locomotive works

At first glance, the steam locomotive may seem a complex machine, and in many ways it can be. However, in other ways it is really very simple – in fact, all locomotives, no matter what their type, can be divided into four basic sections:

1 **The boiler** – which contains the water and is heated to create the steam needed for propulsion.
2 **The engine** – the cylinders and motion that use the steam generated to create a rotational force.
3 **The frames and wheels** – the 'chassis' of our locomotive, upon which every other component is carried.
4 **The 'fuel tank'** – the storage facility for the water and the combustion material burnt to heat the water. This is generally coal, although it can also be wood or oil. The facility comprises either tanks on the loco, or a tender, which is a truck hauled directly behind the locomotive itself.

OPPOSITE Great Western Railway No 4953 *Pitchford Hall*, **seen visiting Crewe Loco Works for an open day, is a 4-6-0 tender locomotive built in 1932.** *(Eddie Bellass)*

In this part of the book, we will study each section in turn. Before we do that, however, we must ensure that we describe our locomotive correctly, which basically means learning about wheel arrangements.

The accepted format for describing a locomotive is: leading truck, coupled driving wheels and trailing truck. In the UK the wheels on both sides of the loco are counted, so for example, a small tank engine with just three driving wheels on each side is classed as an 0-6-0. A large express loco such as *Flying Scotsman*, which has a four-wheeled leading truck (or 'bogie'), and a two-wheeled trailing (pony) truck, is designated 4-6-2.

On the Continent however, locomotives are defined by their axles, rather than wheels, so in France, *Flying Scotsman* would be a 2-3-1 while in Germany, letters are used for the driving axles, turning the *Scotsman* into a 2-C-1.

Just to add a further complication, the more popular wheel arrangements have gained names over the years. A 4-6-2, for example, is known as a Pacific, hence 'the famous Pacific locomotive *Flying Scotsman*'.

The accompanying table shows the major wheel arrangements and their names.

The other important aspect to consider before we delve into the technical details of steam locomotives is their track gauge – the space between the rails. As previously mentioned, approximately 60 per cent of railways around the world have been built to what is known as standard gauge – 4ft 8½in (1,435mm). The origins of this seemingly less than obvious figure are hazy, but it is generally accepted that the earliest waggonways with crude rails set the wheels of their wagons around 5ft (1,500mm) apart so as to fit a horse, the motive power, between the wagon shafts.

Early colliery railways in the north of England used various gauges ranging from 4ft to 5ft (1,200–1,500mm). Pioneer railwayman George Stephenson, who worked around the collieries, chose a gauge of 4ft 8in (1,422mm) when he built the Stockton & Darlington Railway, opened in 1825 and regarded as the pioneer of successful locomotive-powered railways. But when Stephenson built the world's first official passenger railway, between the cities of Liverpool and Manchester, opened in 1830, he added an extra half inch to the gauge to

UK (Whyte)	France	Germany	Name
0-4-0	0-2-0	B	**Four-coupled**
0-6-0	0-3-0	C	**Six-coupled**
0-8-0	0-4-0	D	**Eight-coupled**
2-4-0	1-2-0	1-B	Porter
0-4-2	0-2-1	B-1	
2-6-0	1-3-0	1-C	**Mogul**
0-6-2	0-3-1	C-1	
2-4-2	1-2-1	1-B-1	Columbia
2-6-2	1-3-1	1-C-1	**Prairie**
4-4-0	2-2-0	2-B	American
0-4-4	0-2-2	B-2	Forney
4-4-2	2-2-1	2-B-1	**Atlantic**
2-6-4	1-3-2	1-C-2	**Adriatic**
4-6-0	2-3-0	2-C	Ten-wheel
4-6-2	2-3-1	2-C-1	**Pacific**
2-8-2	1-4-1	1-D-1	**Mikado**
2-10-0	1-5-0	1-E	**Decapod**

LEFT This diagram shows the more common locomotive wheel arrangements. In the UK the Whyte notation has always been used, as devised by Frederick Methvan Whyte, a Dutch engineer working in the USA in 1900. The French and German terms are shown, along with their names where applicable (those used in the UK are in bold).

reduce wheel binding on curves. The Liverpool & Manchester was phenomenally successful, Stephenson and his son Robert as a result, were contracted to construct further lines, building them to the same gauge, and 'standard gauge' was born.

Standard gauge was, however, by no means universal. Isambard Kingdom Brunel, Chief Engineer of the Great Western Railway (GWR), created the 7ft ¼in (2,140mm) broad gauge. This had advantages over the standard gauge, particularly in terms of stability of trains at speed, and the space within the carriages. However, Brunel's grand scheme was out of step with the far more rapidly growing standard gauge, creating problems particularly of offloading and reloading freight when it was transferred between the GWR and connecting carriers. Eventually, the broad gauge was abandoned, the last GWR service running in 1892.

In some countries, a 'broader' standard gauge survives today – all mainline railways in Ireland, for example, are built to 5ft 3in (1,600mm) gauge. Then there is the narrow gauge.

Technically, narrow gauge is anything less than 4ft 8½in, and the appeal of the narrow gauge to many railway builders was its cheapness. This enabled railways to be built without, for example, major earthworks such as cuttings, embankments and tunnels – they simply went up hills and down the other side. So the traditional image of the narrow gauge is a line of sharp curves, steep gradients and small trains. Generally, such lines are of 3ft 6in (1,067mm) gauge or less, the most popular being the 'two foot', the description actually covering various gauges within a couple of inches of 2ft (610mm)! In some cases these are as narrow as 15 inches (380mm), but under this gauge lines are normally classified as miniature railways.

ABOVE This 'Terrier' tank locomotive built in 1872 for the London, Brighton & South Coast Railway and today preserved on the Bluebell Railway in East Sussex, has an 0-6-0 wheel arrangement.

ABOVE A good example of a narrow gauge steam loco. *Prince* was built in 1863 for the Ffestiniog Railway and has been running trains on its 1ft 11½in gauge track (known colloquially as 'the two foot') ever since. *(Courtesy Ffestiniog Railway)*

RIGHT Narrow gauge design follows few common rules. The Romanian Resita 0-8-0T, left, and the Barclay 0-4-0T gasworks tank *Dougal,* right, run on the same 2ft 6in gauge track.

Narrow gauge, however, follows few rules. In some countries, such as South Africa and India, vast mainline systems were built to 3ft 6in or 1 metre (39in) gauge. Also in South Africa for example, similar mainline systems were built using a gauge as narrow as 2ft (610mm), reaching many hundreds of miles and operated by enormous, powerful locomotives. The accompanying photograph (below left) depicts the variety of the narrow gauge – both locomotives running on the same track.

A (mildly) technical description of the steam locomotive

The good news for anyone aspiring to working on a steam locomotive footplate is that you do not need to have the equivalent of a university degree in the workings of said locomotive. A basic knowledge of its working parts is, however, highly desirable, particularly in understanding why it behaves in a certain way, and at certain times.

You will also find that the more you learn about the workings of locomotives, the more you will want to know, which is not a bad thing.

Indeed, many heritage railways run training sessions on various aspects of locomotives and their handling to impart such knowledge to the next generation of footplate crews and ensure this skill is preserved. These sessions are known as Mutual Improvement Classes – which is exactly what they were called in the days when steam ruled the mainlines.

The boiler

While many descriptions of locomotives start with the frames, it is of course, the boiler that produces the steam which provides the power for locomotion. Whatever the size and type of the locomotive, boiler design follows broadly similar principles.

A boiler consists basically of a tube, usually made of steel, and attached at the front to the smokebox, and at the rear to the firebox. The boiler barrel is usually made up of flat mild steel plates, of around 3–6ft (900–1,800mm) wide and ½in to ¾in (13–20mm) thick, which are rolled into rings which are then riveted or welded together. The only major design difference is that in earlier locos, and smaller engines such as shunting, industrial or narrow-gauge types, the boiler barrel was built in

LEFT A standard-gauge boiler and firebox, pictured at the Llangollen Railway. The firebox has a sloping ash pan at the base and the boiler has a tapered barrel.

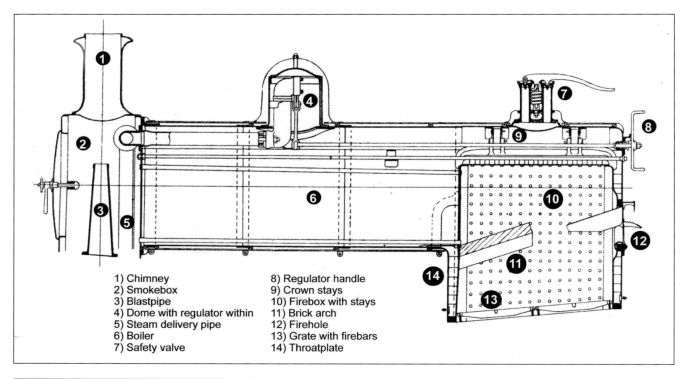

1) Chimney
2) Smokebox
3) Blastpipe
4) Dome with regulator within
5) Steam delivery pipe
6) Boiler
7) Safety valve

8) Regulator handle
9) Crown stays
10) Firebox with stays
11) Brick arch
12) Firehole
13) Grate with firebars
14) Throatplate

ABOVE The layout of a typical boiler.

parallel, whereas in larger, later engines the barrel tapers, being narrower at the front.

This design was one of the innovations of G.J. Churchward, Chief Mechanical Engineer of the Great Western Railway between 1902 and 1922, and it has a number of advantages. It allows a clearer view of the road ahead from the footplate, it reduces the amount of water that can surge to the front of the boiler when the locomotive is going downhill, thus cutting the risk of uncovering the top of the firebox and overheating the boiler. The lower weight at the engine's front end compensates for the heavy cylinders, making it easier to ensure each axle carries an equal weight loading.

When you look at a locomotive from the outside you do not actually see the boiler itself. The boiler barrel is encased in lagging

LEFT This view of Stanier 'Black Five' No 45407 leaving Manchester Victoria in December 2006, shows many boiler fittings, including the short squat, chimney and dome of a large locomotive, and the top-feed. The safety valves are lifting to release excess steam pressure. *(Eddie Bellass)*

to help keep heat in. This was once asbestos but these days the health issues surrounding asbestos have resulted in glassfibre matting being generally used. Thin steel sheets are then wrapped around the lagging to keep it in place and dry, and these are secured by thin steel bands. These are often an area of 'bright work' worthy of special attention during cleaning, which is the first task you will learn when you join the footplate department.

Running through the boiler are a number of steel tubes, secured at the front to a circular tubeplate effectively dividing the boiler from the smokebox, and at the rear to the front end of the firebox.

These tubes take the hot gases from the fire through the boiler, heating the water around them, and they also take exhaust smoke and ash to the smokebox. Depending on the size of the locomotive there can be more than 150 boiler tubes, typically all of the same diameter, about 2in (50mm) for a mainline engine. However, if the locomotive is superheated, which we will look at shortly, there will also be up to 20 flue tubes, measuring up to 6in (150mm) in diameter, and located at the top of the 'nest' of tubes. These provide space in which to place the superheater elements.

Boiler tubes are very much life-limited items. Boilers are approved for use by gaining a 'ticket' from a qualified boiler inspector, and while they will typically be inspected every year (usually by an inspector on behalf of the operator's insurance company), the ticket expires every ten years. At this point the boiler requires a full inspection normally involving dismantling the locomotive and lifting the boiler from the frames. While the boiler will not necessarily need replacing at this point, re-tubing will often take place.

BELOW Here, a boiler is being retubed on the Welshpool & Llanfair Light Railway. Some of the old tubes are seen in the foreground.

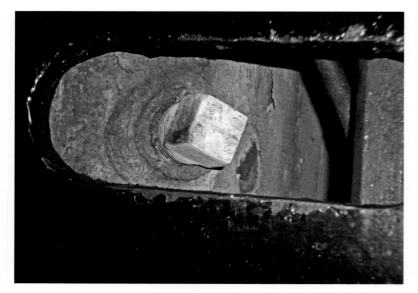

ABOVE A washout plug, in this case bolted into the firebox. Plugs of this type are fitted throughout the locomotive boiler and firebox.

during the overhaul had been slightly too long and projected too far into the firebox – as a result they overheated and eventually cracked.

Throughout the boiler one will find a number of plugs, each having a square head and a tapered thread. These are known as washout plugs and are mostly placed around the firebox, others being located at the smokebox tubeplate end of the boiler. There are also larger versions, known as mudhole doors, placed around the corners of the firebox allowing internal inspection of the box. All are removed to allow access to the inside of the boiler during the washout process, a chore that has to be carried out after a certain number of days running to remove any rubbish, such as scale, that has built up in the boiler. This is very much like the furring that takes place when a kettle is used many times.

Tubes can require replacing at much shorter intervals, usually through wastage or leaking. I know of one locomotive that suffered a spate of leaking tubes just three years after a full overhaul, and eventually was completely re-tubed well before the ten years were up. The suspected cause was that the tubes fitted

Clearly, leaving this in the boiler could have serious consequences for blocking pipes and the like. Most locomotives are given a treatment in their feed water to help loosen this scale from the metal surfaces, and many are 'blown down' at the start or the end of the day to shift the scale. We will look at this further in the firing section.

A small number of the plugs are fitted with a hollow core, which is filled with molten lead alloy and this is allowed to cool. These are the fusible plugs, which are usually located in the top of the firebox and high on the front tubeplate, and are an important safety measure guarding against boiler explosions. Should for example, a shortage of water uncover the top or 'crown' of the firebox, causing it to overheat, the lead in the fusible plug will melt, causing a rush of water and steam into the firebox, warning the crew to drop the fire immediately.

The major protective device for the boiler is the safety valve – or valves, most engines for full protection having two and some large locos four. This is, as its name suggests, a valve placed on the top of the boiler, and designed to open at a certain steam pressure – this is known as lifting or 'blowing off'. By doing so, it prevents too much pressure building in the boiler with the threat of an explosion.

Early safety valves were of the Ramsbottom type, which used a spring and washer arrangement. The spring was held in place by a large overhead lever which projected through

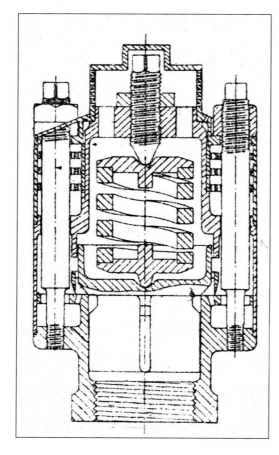

RIGHT A Pop-type safety valve.

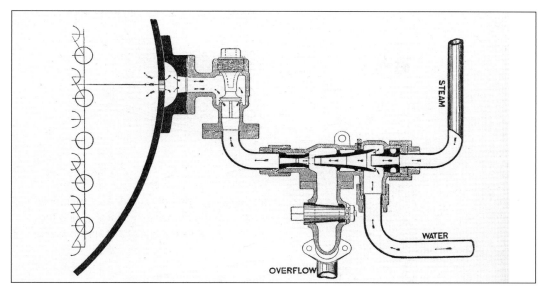

the front of the cab and could be manually operated by the driver if necessary. However, these were almost entirely superseded by the far more efficient Pop safety valve. This 'pops' open and shut far more quickly and is far shorter than the Ramsbottom version.

A boiler full of steam requires constant feeding with water. The earliest locos used an axle-driven feed pump, which was not very efficient, and was entirely superseded by valves known as the injectors, the first of these being patented in July 1858 by Frenchman André Giffard. All locomotives have two injectors, or an injector and a pump, as a situation where

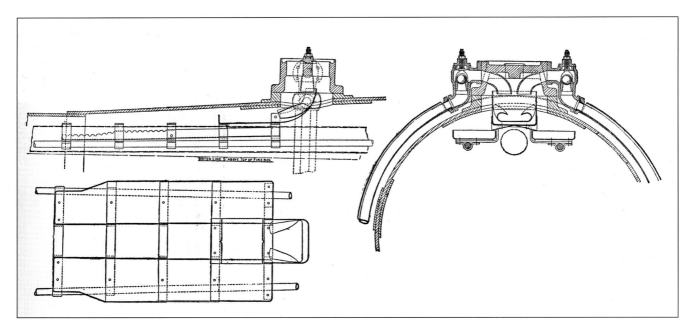

ABOVE The top-feed
system for routing
water into the boiler,
as devised by
GWR engineer
G.J. Churchward.

the only method of getting water into the boiler failed would be potentially catastrophic.

The problem that the injector solves is to put water into the boiler against the pressure of the steam being generated within it. To do this a jet of steam flows into the injector and into a specially shaped cone, which increases the steam flow to very high speed. It discharges into a conical water space, the water condensing the steam and the force generated overcoming the pressure in the boiler.

There are various kinds of injectors, some of which only use live steam taken directly from the boiler, while some also use exhaust steam taken from the smokebox. Usually they are placed under the footplate of the engine, the advantages being that water can be admitted from above, 'flooding' the injector and not having to be lifted. By being placed away from the boiler the injector does not get so hot, as it works more efficiently when cooler. Even so, efficient use of the injector can be one of the more challenging jobs for the fireman, particularly on smaller locos, as we will see later.

The feed water passes from the injectors into the boiler by the clack valves. These are non-return valves mounted on top of the boiler, which close automatically when the injectors are shut off. G.J. Churchward devised the top-feed system which, by routing feed water around the boiler on its way to the clacks, heats it and

thus reduces the change of temperature when it enters the boiler. His method was generally adopted by locomotive designers.

The firebox

Before following the passage of steam through to where it does its job of work, let's look at the two boxes at either end of the boiler, the first providing the heat source. The firebox is actually two boxes, one placed inside the other. The outer firebox is joined directly to the boiler tube and thus provides a jacket of water around the inner firebox, within which is contained the fire.

Around the base the two boxes are joined to each other by a steel bar known as the foundation ring. Another ring between the two at the rear provides the firehole, through which the fire is generally fed, while around all four sides and the top of the two boxes run a great many securing bolts, known as stays. Those at the top are known as crown stays (see diagram).

Depending on their location, stays can be copper or steel, and they will be joined to the inner and outer fireboxes either by screwing and riveting over, or welding. These stays are another critical point in judging the health or otherwise of a boiler during inspections. Leaking stays, often caused by cracking, are a perennial problem in steam locomotive maintenance. Some later designs

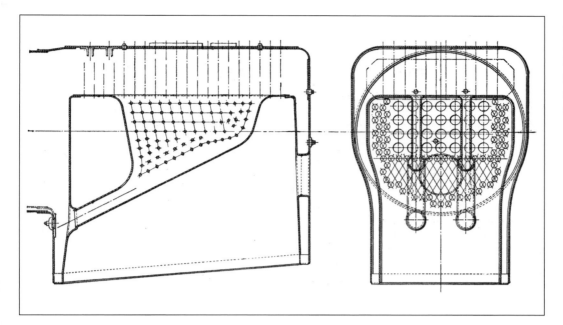

of locomotives also include a pair of large pipes passing diagonally through the firebox from the boiler. These provide extra heating surfaces and are known as thermic siphons.

While the outer firebox is usually made from steel, the inner box can be formed from steel or copper. Usually, just one sheet of metal is used to form the sides and the roof, or crown, of the firebox. In early days the crown was semi-circular but that man Churchward again introduced a more efficient design, this having a flat crown and sides that sloped outwards. This produced a larger heating area at the top of the box, where naturally rising heat would have the greatest effect, and while more difficult to attach to the boiler, it was simpler to brace with stays. This is known as a Belpaire firebox because it was invented by the Belgian, Alfred Belpaire, Churchward merely taking advantage of it for his Great Western engines.

At the front of the inner firebox is the tubeplate, from which the boiler tubes run to the smokebox, while at the base is the grate, on which the fire itself is built. Grates can

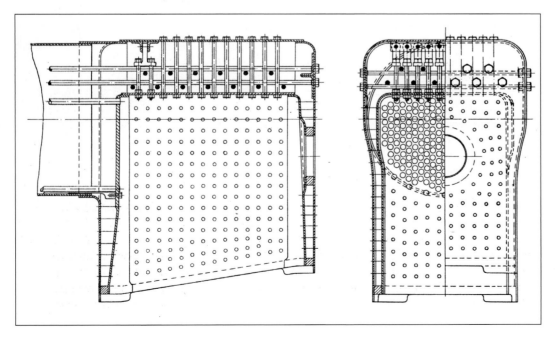

ABOVE In this view of a Belpaire firebox the shape and the heads of the many stays used to hold it together can be seen.

operated the plates rock to an almost vertical position, dropping the remains of an old fire into the ash pan. This is a job of moments, much appreciated by the fireman.

The ash pan is, as its name suggests, a large tray to catch the ash that falls through the grate from the fire. This prevents ash, including hot coals, falling directly on to the track, and running the risk of lineside fires. A typical ash pan will be fitted with a means of disposing of the ash, for example, a side door or a cab-operated floor release. The pan will also boast doors on the front and rear, these being the dampers which are used to create an air path through to the fire.

A more complex version of the ash pan is the hopper type. In some ways it is like a rocking grate with a lever found on the floor of the cab (into which normally slots a steel extension lever) which opens doors on the base of the ash pan, dumping its contents into a pit under the rails, usually in a single operation.

Many fireboxes include a brick arch, which slopes upwards and backwards from just above the fire. Literally made form firebricks, it helps provide more efficient heat generation, principally by forcing the heat created at the front of the fire, to flow back over the fire before entering the boiler tubes. It also keeps the flames away from the boiler tubes and their tubeplate.

The firebox is fed through the firehole in its rear surface, which is sealed by doors. These

be made in various ways, the most simple consisting of a line of bow-shaped firebars made from cast iron. These can be lifted out individually to help drop the ash of an old fire below and into the ash pan.

More complex versions include the rocking grate, which consists of a series of plates linked to a lever in the cab. When the lever is

RIGHT A grate and ash pan showing two rows of bow-shaped firebars, and the front and rear ash pan damper doors with their associated linkage.

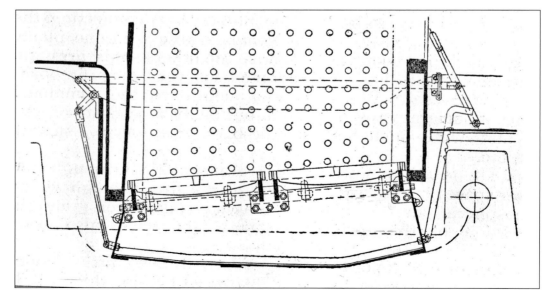

OIL FIRING

An alternative to coal firing a locomotive is the burning of fuel oil. Such methods are used extensively in some countries where oil is rather more plentiful than coal. Immediately following the Second World War, a shortage of coal in the UK saw a programme intending to convert 1,200 locomotives to oil firing. Some 93 had been converted when the government realised it could not afford to import foreign oil, and the converted locos were changed back to coal within nine months.

Similarly, the narrow-gauge Ffestiniog Railway in North Wales converted most of its steam fleet to oil in the 1970s. Initially this was to avoid sparks starting lineside fires in its heavily wooded surroundings. Most of these locomotives have more recently been converted back to coal.

In an oil-fired locomotive the oil is taken from a tank into the firebox, passing through valves and a filter (during which it is heated to increase its fluidity), to the burner. This is mounted in a trough at the base of a small chamber in front of the firebox, and fed by air from below, regulated by dampers as on a coal-fired engine. The burner atomises the oil and injects it into the firebox. Oil fires burn at higher temperatures than coal versions, so the firebox is lined at its base with firebricks to protect the metal, and heat-resisting paint often has to be used on the loco smokebox.

There are several advantages with oil-fired locomotives. The oil fire is very easy to control, it does not produce dust and a dirty footplate, the fireman has much less to do and can therefore aid the driver, for example looking out for signals. As the firehole door is not opened, working after dark there will be no problem of the glare momentarily blinding the footplate crew.

come in various forms, but the most common are twin sliding doors operated by a single lever. Below or behind these doors is normally fitted a baffle, a plate that can be raised to partly cover the fire, allowing cold air to get to a fire that needs calming a little, while also protecting against a fire 'blowing back' on to the footplate, as described in the firing section.

The smokebox

The smokebox is located at the opposite end to the boiler to the firebox, and the opposite the end of the steam path. Having done its work in the cylinders, steam will be directed through the smokebox and then out through the locomotive's chimney by means of a nozzle known as the blastpipe.

LEFT This ash pan fitted to a narrow-gauge locomotive has a side-opening door to enable simple cleaning out of the ash.

RIGHT **This view of GWR 'Manor' class 4-6-0 *Bradley Manor* on the Severn Valley Railway shows the smokebox with its side-swinging door and its two securing levers.**

The smokebox is accessed through a large door in its front, typically dished for greater strength. This is there to allow the smokebox interior to be inspected (particularly the tubeplate, its tube ends and the fusible plugs), and to clean out ash from the box and the tubes, the latter achieved using a very long rod with a brush on the end.

The traditional door is hinged at the side and has a rod passing through it at the centre with a flat end and known as a dart. When turned through 90 degrees using one of two outside handles, this dart catches on a bar inside securing the door. The second lever runs on a thread and is used to tighten the door as a tight seal is essential to maintain the vacuum inside the smokebox and encourage the steam passing through the blast pipe to draw the hot gases through the boiler tubes. There are other types of securing methods for the smokebox door, one much favoured on the Continent being a ring of 'dog-catches' around the edge of the door.

Opening the smokebox door one will normally see the spark arrestor, a large grille – sometimes flat, sometimes box-shaped –

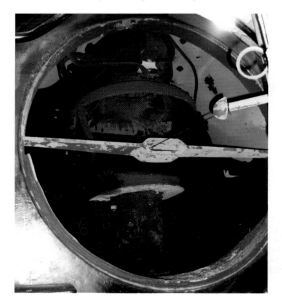

RIGHT The view inside a standard-gauge locomotive smokebox. The D-shaped dart is on the right, which locates in the bar at centre and is turned to secure it. Behind it is the locomotive's blast pipe, surrounded by a spark arrestor.

which as its name suggests is designed to catch hot particles and prevent lineside fires. Also visible is the blast pipe, which will also have the blower pipe attached. The blower is a means available to the fireman to encourage his fire by directing a jet of steam up the blastpipe thus increasing the drawing of hot gases through the boiler.

The design of the blast pipe, and for that matter the chimney (not, as it is sometimes incorrectly called, the 'funnel' – you find those on ocean liners!), is important to encourage the most efficient exhaust and pull on the fire. Several blast pipe designs have been developed over the years, one of the most modern designs being the Lempor exhaust. Designed by Argentinian Livio Dante Porta in 1952, it has in the eyes of many, succeeded the Kylchap exhaust, produced by Frenchman André Chapelon in 1925, as the most efficient. Its design creates a vacuum in one cylinder as the other ejects its used steam, thus requiring less pressure to drive the piston. This has been claimed to add as much as 40 per cent more power to a locomotive.

Behind all this is the front tubeplate with the ends of the boiler tubes visible for inspection, and if needed, cleaning. There will also be fusible plugs visible here.

Superheating

Superheating was a major advance in locomotive design from the early 20th century, and became an almost standard fitment in later locomotives, particularly larger standard-gauge examples. In short, superheating further heats the steam generated in the boiler before sending it to the cylinders. This makes the loco more efficient as the steam has more thermal energy and is less likely to condense back to water on its route to the cylinders, which could be disastrous, as we will see shortly.

To convert normal steam, known as saturated or wet steam, to superheated steam, after being collected in the dome it is passed back and forth through the boiler within special pipes, known as superheater elements. These are placed inside wider flue tubes which are located at the top of the boiler and carry hot gases just like the normal boiler tubes.

Travelling from the superheater header at the front tubeplate, the steam normally loops back on itself twice at the firebox end and once at the smokebox end, therefore travelling four times extra through the boiler before being directed to the cylinders.

Placing superheater elements inside the flue tubes runs the risk of them melting in the hot temperatures. Steam passing through them cools these elements sufficiently to prevent damage, but when the loco is coasting and no steam is being used another method has to be employed. Some locos use a snifting valve, which is normally mounted behind the chimney, which allows air into the superheater elements to cool them when not under power.

LEFT These are superheater flues removed from a locomotive during overhaul. Note how they loop back on themselves at the far end.

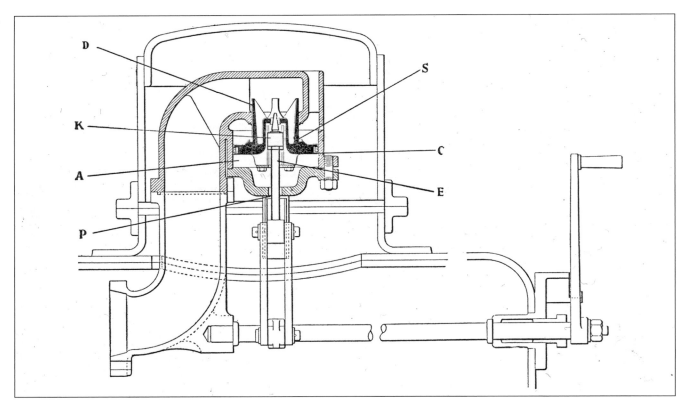

ABOVE A regulator,
in this case mounted
in the locomotive's
steam dome.

The engine

We now need to follow the path of the steam generated in the boiler to its place of work, the cylinders – effectively, the engine of the locomotive. Steam is taken from the top of the boiler and collected, usually (but not always) in a dome mounted on top of the boiler barrel and usually around its centre point. On smaller standard-gauge and narrow-gauge locos these domes can be quite tall and distinctive, but on larger UK locomotives the dome tends to be a squat item, due to the restrictions placed on its dimensions by the loading gauge of British railways.

The dome is a popular place to mount the controls for the locomotive's regulator – its 'accelerator', although these controls can also be mounted in the smokebox. From the dome the steam is piped directly to the cylinders, or is looped back and forth along the large flue tubes to superheat it before it enters the cylinders.

The cylinders

The cylinders are the essential power plant creating the back-and-forth movement which the motion (see page 50) will convert to a radial motion to move the locomotive. In almost all locomotives the cylinders are mounted at the front end, neatly counterbalancing the weight of the firebox at the rear end.

General locomotive practice calls for two, three or four cylinders. The simplest layout, common on tank and narrow gauge engines, is for two cylinders mounted outside the frames. Some engines have two cylinders inside the frames, while larger more powerful locos will be fitted with two outside cylinders supplemented by one or two between the frames.

A cylinder is, as its name suggests, a tube closed off at both ends, with a piston and rod running inside it. The disc of the piston contains cast-iron piston rings which ensure it remains steam tight against the inside cylinder wall. Steam is admitted at one end of the cylinder, forcing the piston along the tube, and is then exhausted. When the piston reaches the end of its stroke, known as 'dead centre', steam is admitted behind it, forcing it back the other way.

The cylinders on either side of the locomotive are set up 90 degrees of a wheel revolution apart, known as quartering, ensuring there is always some degree of pushing occurring on one side of the motion, while the other side is

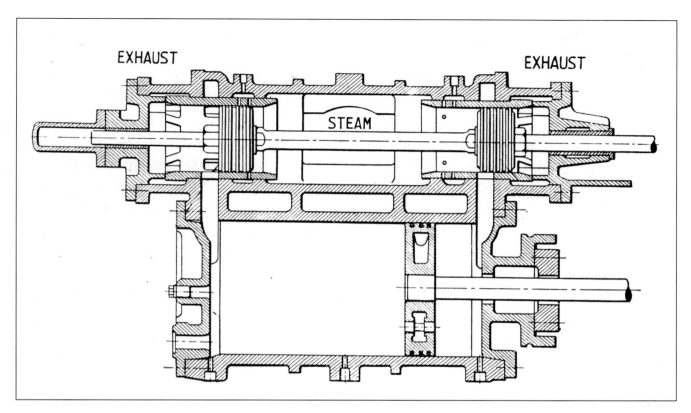

EXHAUST   EXHAUST

STEAM

in its exhaust cycle, thus preventing the motion from locking up.

The admission to and exit of steam from the cylinders is controlled by valves, mounted either between or on the top of the cylinders in what are known as the steamchests. These valves are actuated by rods that form part of the valve gear, as we'll see later.

The valves can generally be of two types, either slide or piston. Generally, slide valves were used in locomotives built throughout the 19th century but were then gradually superseded by piston valves.

The slide valve is effectively a flat, boxed-shape casting that moves over the ports cut into the side of the cylinder, alternatively opening and closing those ports and letting steam in and out of the cylinder. Steam is admitted from the outside of the valve, which is known as outside admission.

The slide valve is also often called a D-valve because if you were to cut it in half, the inside profile of the casting loosely resembles the letter D. This design provides a chamber for steam to collect in as it is exhausted from the cylinder. From this chamber the exhaust steam passes to the blastpipe and chimney.

ABOVE A piston-valve cylinder. The movement of the valve pistons at the top uncover the ports admitting and exhausting steam into/from the cylinder itself and moving its piston.

BELOW This cylinder is of the older slide-valve variety with the flat plate slide valve at the top uncovering the ports to admit and exhaust steam.

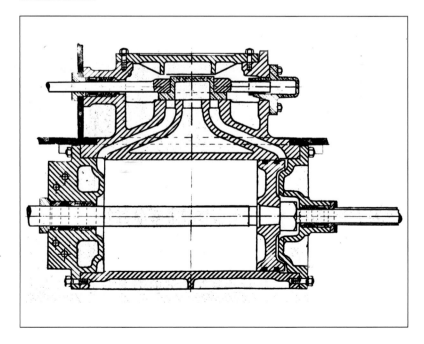

RIGHT A slide valve in action. At the upper left the piston is at the end of its stroke and the slide valve open to 'lead'. At the lower left the piston has travelled halfway to the point of cut-off and the valve is open to allow maximum steam in. At upper right the piston has reached cut-off and the valve closes. The piston continues to travel to the end of its stroke, lower right, where the port opens to exhaust and the port at the other end closes, allowing compression.

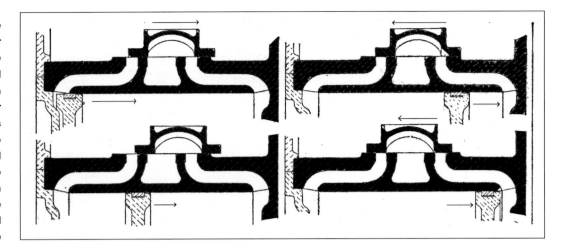

RIGHT A diagram showing a typical slide valve and its buckle, which is joined to the valve rod of the motion. Note the interior cut-out which gives it the nickname of 'D-valve'.

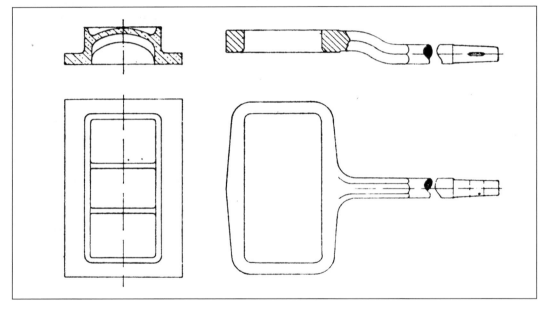

RIGHT A diagram illustrating a piston valve.

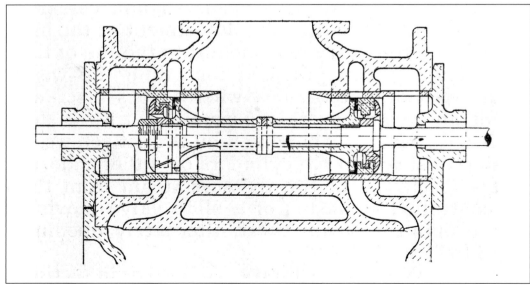

The piston valve is of similar design to the piston in the cylinder. It has two circular heads mounted on a single spindle in a cylindrical steam chest, and these move up and down opening and closing ports to the cylinder and again, letting steam in and out.

The piston valve is regarded as more efficient than the slide valve because the pressure acting on one piston balances that of the other, therefore these valves can be more accurately set. While piston valves can be of outside admission, generally they are inside admission, injecting the steam between the pistons, and is favoured particularly with superheated steam.

Due to its higher pressures in an outside-admission design such steam would place great strain on the point where the valve spindle exits the steam chest, known as a stuffing box. In an inside-admission design the stuffing box is exposed only to low-pressure exhaust steam. Generally, piston valves are a more complex design than the slide valve and overall, the latter design was used by more locomotives.

There is a third, much less-common type of valve, the poppet valve. These were used in Caprotti valve gear, as fitted to a few BR Standard engines, and described later. The poppet valve is operated by a cam, and is effectively a development of the systems used in the internal combustion engines of cars.

An important phrase in relation to the valves is lap and lead. To make the cylinder work more efficiently, the valve overlaps the steam port at the middle of the stroke. This is called lap and there are two types, which can be varied depending on the job of work required of the engine. Steam lap is by how much the valve covers the live steam admission port, while exhaust lap is the equivalent on the steam exhaust port. Exhaust lap is more common on slow-running locos built for heavy hauling as it ensures the steam stays in the cylinder for as long as possible before exiting, making the loco a more efficient hauler.

Lead is how much the live steam port is permitted to be open at the end of the piston stroke, when it comes to a halt at either the front or back of the cylinder. By admitting steam to fill the space between the piston and cylinder end, pressure is increased to aid the beginning of the next stoke. This is a very useful feature on fast-running locomotives, where pistons and valves are moving very rapidly.

Also mounted on the cylinders will be found small valves, controlled from the cab and known as drain cocks. These carry out an essential function. If a locomotive is standing for any length of time any steam in the cylinders will cool and condense back to water. By opening the drain cocks before moving off, the driver uses new steam to blow this water safely out of the cylinders through the cocks. While adding to the drama of a loco moving off from a stand, this action also provides essential safety as without these cocks, the piston would compress the water into the end of the cylinder causing extensive damage and even risking blowing the end of the cylinder clean off.

The motion

The complex scientific formulae that have created the various types of motion fitted to steam locomotives can easily fill entire books of their own, and indeed many learned tomes have been written about even individual systems. But as we said at the start of this chapter, you can have a perfectly healthy working relationship with a steam locomotive without needing to know all the theories behind the actions of the many variants of motion employed over the years, such as Stephenson's Link, Walschaerts, and Joy. What you do need to know is what the system is basically required to do and how it does it, which is the level we explore here.

BELOW This narrow-gauge 2-6-2T, built by Hunslet in 1954 for work in Sierra Leone, is seen on the Welshpool & Llanfair Light Railway with its cylinder drain cocks open and exhausting steam from the front, along with any condensed water.

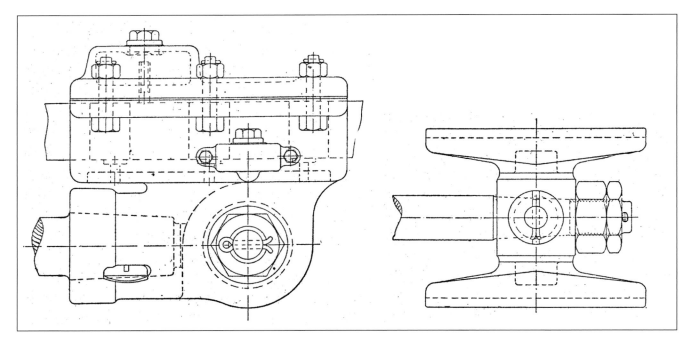

If however, you do find the subject enthusing and want to know more, some suggested further reading will be found at the back of the book.

While many enthusiasts refer to the complete layout of rods and cranks as the 'valve gear', this is actually only the part that operates the valves in the steam ports. Railwaymen tend to refer to the whole setup as the 'motion'. This can be mounted almost entirely inside the frames, entirely outside the frames or, commonly, with the motion mounted outside the frames and the valve gear between the frames.

No matter how complex its form, the motion performs two basic and opposite functions. It converts the back-and-forth movement of the piston into a radial movement to propel the locomotive, and it converts that radial movement back to a forward-and-back motion to operate the valves on the inlet and exhaust steam ports on the cylinder, thus providing the means to create the next radial movement, and so on.

The motion also performs effectively the same function as a gearbox in a car, varying the amount of torque, or pulling power, related to speed. By altering the geometry of the motion, the driver can provide much greater pulling power (for moving a train away from a standstill, for example) and then, as the locomotive increases speed, he can reduce the difference between power and speed to suit. This is rather like one goes up through the gears from first to fifth or more in a car.

Finally, by pulling back on the reversing lever (reverser) the driver can alter the geometry to such an extent that it reacts in the opposite direction, thus reversing the engine. However, the difference in a car gearbox and a locomotive's

LEFT The cylinder end of a locomotive with Walschaerts motion. The vertical combination lever operates the valve gear. The crosshead and the piston rod enter the cylinder through the stuffing box. Note the oil filler on top of the upper slide bar.

reversing lever is that the loco driver has a full range of gears available whether running in forward or reverse, because many locomotives, particularly tank locos, are expected to be as efficient in reverse as when running forwards.

No matter which type of valve gear employed (and we will look at some of the more popular designs shortly), the basics remain the same. The pistons are mounted at one end of rods which move in and out of the cylinder (just as on the valve chests, the point at which they exit is known as a stuffing box). The piston rod is joined at the other end to a commonly H-shaped plate – the crosshead. This slides between two guides mounted above and/or below the rear of the cylinder, which are known as the slide bars.

From the crosshead a long steel rod, the connecting rod, leads to the driving wheels. On a four-coupled locomotive it is usually connected to the rearmost of the two largest pairs of wheels. On locos with six main driving wheels or more, the connecting rod can be connected to the rearmost, but more usually, is mounted on either the centre, or in the case of locos of eight driving wheels, either of the centre pair of wheels. These large wheels are joined together by another rod, the coupling rod, the driving wheels thus being known as coupled wheels – hence the expression four-coupled, six-coupled loco and the like.

The coupling rod transfers the motion generated by the connecting rod to the other wheels and while called a coupling rod in the singular, it often comes in more than one part

LEFT The end of a locomotive rod with its bearing, which comes in two halves.

to allow a little flexibility on curves. Both the connecting and coupling rods have brass bearings at their extremities, which as a result, are known as 'ends'. On the connecting rod the little end joins to the crosshead and the big end to the driving wheel. Large steel pins, known as crank pins, run in these bearings and are attached close to the outer rim of the driving wheels, thus providing the propelling force.

That's the easy part! The complex part is where the mechanism to operate the cylinder valves and the mechanism to match power and torque to the train's speed are incorporated.

Stephenson Link motion

The older of the two most popular forms of motion is the Stephenson Link, which is renowned for its simplicity and was much used on locomotives, particularly in the 19th century. As its name suggests it dates back to the time of George Stephenson, but it was two

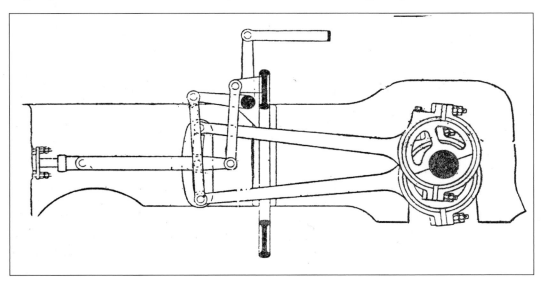

LEFT A simplified view of the workings of the Stephenson Link motion, usually, but not always, mounted between the frames of the locomotive. The eccentrics are linked to the curved, slotted expansion link, whose geometry is changed by the linkage at the top leading to the reverser in the cab.

ABOVE The eccentrics of a locomotive fitted with Stephenson Link motion.

BELOW The valves of Stephenson Link motion, and the top of the expansion links are shown here.

valve travel a shorter distance, therefore varying the valve lap and cutting off steam earlier in the cycle. This provided greater control, depending on what the loco was doing. When starting a train a long valve movement was used, around 80 per cent of the stroke before cut-off, the cut-off shortened as speed and momentum gained and less effort was needed for each stroke. As we have said, this is much like one changes up a gear in a car. The cut-off was controlled by the reversing lever in the cab, which had notches in it for the various positions, leading to the phrase 'notching up'. Also, by varying the valve lap, the system could automatically vary the lead accordingly, adding to the efficiency.

The Stephenson Link motion had some disadvantages, particularly in that its eccentrics produced cramped conditions between the loco frames and the need to move the expansion link required quite a lot of height to work effectively. Daniel Gooch of the GWR, tried to address this problem with his own derivative, and later Alexander Allan came up with a gear combining the Stephenson and Gooch concepts, but while both found some success on the Continent they were little used in the UK. Stephenson Link motion became almost universally used until effectively superseded by Walschaerts motion.

Walschaerts motion

Walschaerts valve gear first found wide acceptance at the start of the 20th century, which was remarkable as it was invented by the Belgian engineer Egide Walschaerts back in 1844! Its major advantage was that it could be mounted either on the inside or, much more commonly, entirely on the outside of the locomotive, thus occupying no space between the frames. This was particularly useful on articulated locomotives, which saw the earliest use of the gear. Once fully understood, the gear became virtually universal on the European railway scene and also the most common gear in America.

Walschaerts gear effectively consists of two major elements. Reference to the drawing will help in understanding its workings. The first is a pair of rods (the union or connecting link and combination lever) connected between the crosshead and the valve spindle. The movement back and forth of the piston and crosshead therefore moves the valve spindle back and forth

employees in his factory who came up with the design in 1841. At the time, most locomotives used Gab motion, which had two axle-mounted eccentrics to power the valves in each cylinder, one for driving the loco forwards and one for backwards. The two eccentric rods had slotted ends, one of which would contact a pin on the valve rod depending on the loco's direction. It was quite a clumsy system which had no means of adjustment.

The two Stephenson workers, William Howe and William Williams, came up with a curved, slotted plate, known as the expansion link to which the two eccentric rods were joined, one at the top and one at the bottom. By means of the reversing lever in the cab this link could be rotated and the change in geometry would not only alter the direction of the engine, but by making smaller alterations could make the

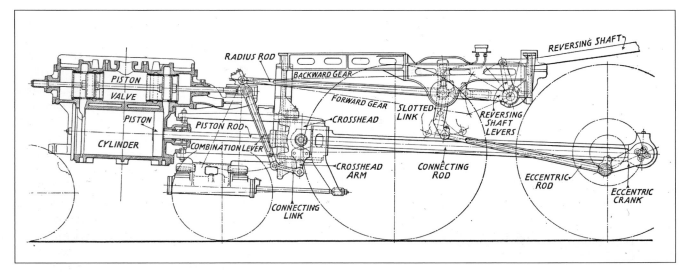

in the steam chests. The movement is equivalent to twice the lap plus the lead of the valve.

The second element consists of a crank mounted on the loco's driving axle, but if the gear is mounted between the frames an eccentric does the same job. The crank revolves around the centre line of the axle at a set radius. The motion it creates is passed through a rod, the eccentric rod, to the bottom of the expansion link that is curved and slotted rather like that in the Stephenson Link motion. However, whereas in Stephenson link motion the entire expansion link can move up and down, in Walschaerts its location is fixed, pivoting centrally about a bracket mounted on the frames. The joint at which it pivots is known as the expansion pivot.

From the rear of the valve spindle another rod, the radius rod, joins to the expansion link

be means of a connection called the die block, which can slide up and down in the expansion link. This movement, controlled from the reversing lever in the cab, alters the geometry of the gear and the position of the valve in the steam chest, thus providing the different levels of power and reversing ability that we have already seen with Stephenson Link motion.

If the die block is positioned at the central point of the expansion link, then the link will not pivot and will not pass on a movement through the radius rod to the valve spindle – this is 'mid gear', or standstill. As the die block moves up or down the expansion link, the amount of movement transmitted to the valves increases, thus controlling the point at which steam is cut off in the cylinder. With the die block close to the centre steam is cut off early, when at either the top or bottom of the link

ABOVE A diagram showing Walschaerts motion as fitted to a 4-6-2 Pacific locomotive, with its various components named. The coupling rods have been omitted for clarity.

BELOW A simplified diagram of Walschaerts motion.

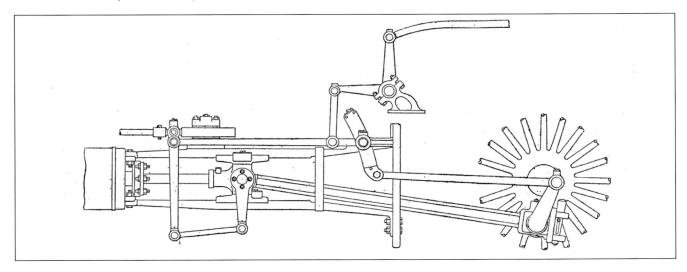

ABOVE Gresley 4-6-2 A4 Pacific *Union of South Africa* shows off its Walschaerts gear. Note the copper pipes of the cylinder drain cocks. *(Eddie Bellass)*

RIGHT These two views show the function of Walschaerts gear. Note the differing position of the radius rod, ringed in the upper picture, when the locomotive is running backwards (above), and forwards (below).

steam is cut off at the last moment possible, for example, when the most power is needed for starting a train.

While complex to describe, the process is quite clear to see by study of the photographs here of Walschaerts-equipped locomotives. It is depicted in forward, and reverse gears and compares the position on the expansion link of the radius rod.

Other types of motion

Stephenson Link and Walschaerts motion have been fitted to the overwhelming majority of locomotives built over the years, but there have been other systems tried which we will look at briefly.

Joy valve gear was patented by engineer David Joy in 1870. It was used extensively on Lancashire & Yorkshire and London & North Western Railway locomotives, several steam traction engines, and the Manning Wardle-built narrow-gauge 2-6-2T locomotives of the Lynton & Barnstaple Railway.

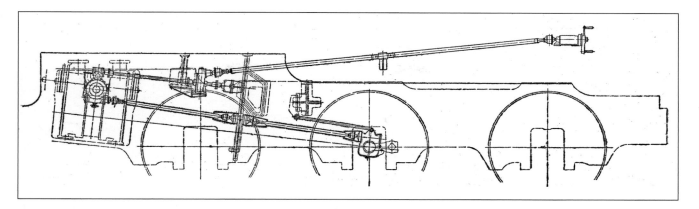

A replica of one of these, *Lyd* entered service at the Ffestiniog Railway in 2010. On the Joy gear a vertical link runs from the connecting rod to a slotted expansion link. Like on Walschaerts the expansion link pivots centrally, but in this case transferring the vertical movement to horizontal movement to propel the valve rods.

Oliver Bulleid, Chief Mechanical Engineer of the Southern Railway between 1937 and 1948, created a chain-drive gear. From the central driving wheel a system of chains ran to a jockey shaft. This shaft was joined with rods running to the expansion links and from them rods ran in traditional form to the valves. Adding further complexity was a pair of small cylinders connected to the reverser in the cab

and designed to help the driver change the gear. The cylinders linked to the design's version of the radius rod. The Bulleid system was controversial and not adopted elsewhere.

Finally in this study we should briefly consider Caprotti valve gear. The youngest of our gears, it was created by Italian Arturo Caprotti following the First World War, but did not see wide use until an improved version was tried, with mixed results, on some British Railways Standard-class locomotives in the 1950s.

As mentioned previously, Caprotti gear draws on automotive practice. The steam valve chest effectively becomes a cambox, in which are fitted Poppet valves operated by cams just like in a car. Caprotti's design

ABOVE A diagram of Caprotti valve gear which uses cams in a similar way to automotive practice.

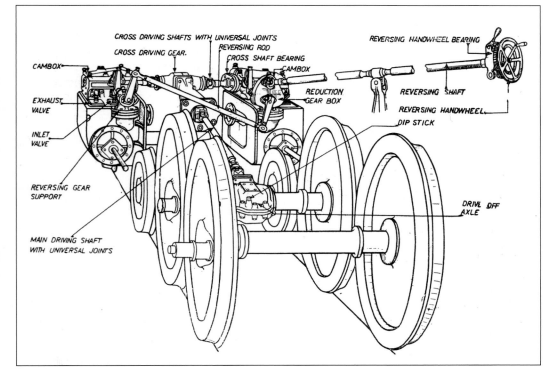

LEFT This perspective view shows how Caprotti valve gear is fitted.

ABOVE British Railways Pacific 4-6-2 No. 71000 *Duke of Gloucester* is the best-known British example of a loco fitted with Caprotti valve gear. *(Eddie Bellass)*

BELOW The frames of a large, standard-gauge locomotive showing the bufferbeam at the front and the vertical rectangular cut-outs for the axleboxes. The lower edge of the frame is raised at the front to allow clearance for the bogie truck.

used two inlet cams and a single exhaust cam, whereas the later British version added a second exhaust cam. The two sets of cams could be moved mechanically in relation to each other changing the timing of the valves, thus providing completely independent control of steam admission and exhaust to the cylinder. Ironically, variable valve timing has only recently come about in the automotive industry, where it has been seen as a great advance.

In Caprotti gear a drive is taken to the cambox by means of shafts from the driving wheel of the locomotive, each shaft joined to the next by universal joints. The design was expensive, but advantages in addition to the variable valve timing included the fact that much of the hardware was enclosed, and so suffered far less wear and tear. The unique BR Standard Class 8 Pacific locomotive No. 71000 *Duke of Gloucester*, built in 1954, was fitted with Caprotti gear but considered a disappointment during its very short British Railways service of

just eight years, being dubbed a poor steamer. It was returned to running order in 1988, and during the restoration significant mistakes in the original construction of its chimney and grate were found and rectified, solving the steaming issues. 'The Duke' has since proven a highly capable locomotive on many mainline steam specials across the UK.

The chassis (the running gear)

Frames

The main frame of a locomotive provides the essential component on to which everything else – the boiler, cylinders, motion, wheels, cab and tanks is attached. The frame members must be rigid and strong as it is on them that the entire structural integrity of the locomotive is based.

On the vast majority of standard-gauge

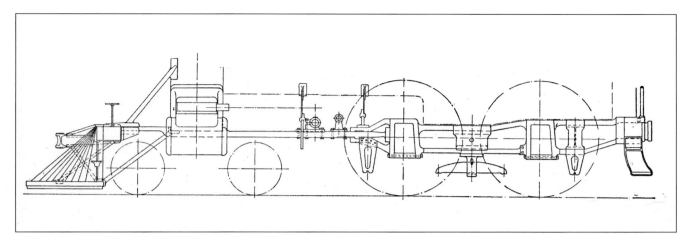

locos the main frame is placed inside the wheels. However, on narrow-gauge locomotives outside framing is far more common because this offers a number of advantages. Principally, you free up more space between the wheels for such essential items as the valve gear, while at the back outside frames allow the use of a wider firebox, this being placed traditionally between the frames. Some inside-frame narrow-gauge engines get over this problem by stopping the main frames short of the firebox and bolting them to it, or bolting them to a wider cradle on which is hung the rear bufferbeam.

The European and US approaches to main frame construction differ markedly. In America, loco frames were constructed from steel bars of some three to four inches (75–100mm) square section, but virtually all locomotives used in Britain and Europe had their frames constructed from steel plate rolled to around a thickness of one inch (25mm).

Frames can vary from the simple rectangular plates of smaller locomotives to complex designs of varying width and height to accommodate trailing and leading wheel trucks.

The two main frame members are joined together in several places, both to provide mounting points for various parts of the locomotive and to add rigidity. It is essential that the frames run true so as not to cause uneven wear and stress in the axle boxes and to ensure correct working of the motion as the slide bars on the cylinders must always be exactly parallel to the line of the piston – again to avoid excessive wear. The lining up

process during construction is carried out to exacting measurements.

The obvious plates joining the two frames together are the front and rear bufferbeams, in the case of tank locomotives, and the front bufferbeam and rear drawbar on a tender locomotive. These are usually of steel plate somewhat thicker than the frames, some variants using two thinner plates sandwiching a core of oak wood and thus giving a little 'springability' reducing the shock when the buffers come together during coupling up.

Along the length of the frames there are various items adding to the rigidity. These include the cylinders, especially if inside cylinders are fitted. If outside cylinders are used then a very firm stay is normally placed between them to compensate for the fore and aft stresses put on the frames by the working of the motion. Where the motion includes valve gear between the frames this will also have a stay, again stiffening matters, while there can also be stretchers placed at various points along the frames.

The boiler, however, does not add to this rigidity. Whilst attached to the footplate (this being the horizontal plate running around the loco, providing the crew with somewhere to stand when accessing various components, more usually referred to as the running plate, and including the floor of the cab), it is in turn attached to the frames at the front, smokebox end, while at the rear both the boiler and its firebox rest on a bar generally made of angle iron. This is to allow some movement of the boiler along its length as it expands and cools under the action of the heat generated within it.

ABOVE The American method of loco frame construction is very different to European in that instead of steel plates, steel bars are employed.

ABOVE In this narrow-gauge locomotive undergoing restoration, the axleboxes can be seen sitting inside hornblocks bolted to the frame. One of the hornblocks can just be seen in the left background on the opposite side of the frame – these are held in place by keeps along their lower edges.

ABOVE RIGHT A locomotive axlebox. The outer edge is stepped to allow it to run in the hornbox and the bearing is in the top half with the lower half forming an oil bath.

RIGHT A diagram of a hornblock and the axlebox that runs within it. The two rods at the bottom will be acted on by the springs.

Axle boxes

From the bottom of the frames wide rectangular cut-outs are provided to accommodate the axle boxes of the coupled wheels. Over these cut-outs are fitted horseshoe-like pieces known as the horn blocks. These were initially made from cast iron, but in later engines, of cast steel, and it is within these that the axle boxes move up and down. They are secured by a keep at the bottom and their movement regulated by the springs.

In the axle boxes are bearings that generally come in two halves, surrounding the axle ends. The top half is made of bronze or brass and lined with whitemetal, which is an alloy containing tin and lead providing a softer surface to bear on the axle, transferring the weight of the loco to it. The bottom half, made of brass or cast iron, effectively forms a bath in which the lubricant for the axles sits. Ensuring the axle box runs smoothly on the axle with no high spots is essential and on many heritage railways you will see workshop staff members performing the tedious but vital role of

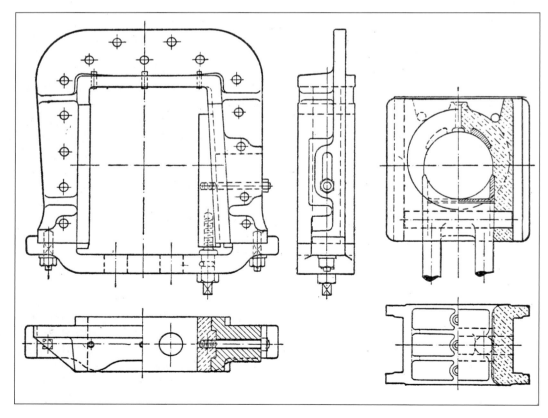

removing slithers of extraneous metal from the bearing using a scraper.

The coupled wheels on most locomotives use leaf springs. These can be located under or over the axle box and consist of up to ten laminated strips of steel increasing in length to, on a large standard-gauge locomotive, around 3ft (914mm). They allow movement of the axle box by approximately one to two inches (25–50mm). Some more recent narrow-gauge locomotives have used pairs of coil springs on

ABOVE LEFT Here, an axlebox bearing is being scraped to ensure the axle itself runs smoothly within it. Blue marking has been used to identify high spots which must be gently scraped away.

ABOVE On this outside-framed locomotive the axlebox can be seen with the leaf spring mounted above it.

their coupled wheels. Generally, however, coil springs are employed in the smaller uncoupled wheels in the bogie or trailing pony trucks.

ARTICULATED LOCOMOTIVES

Traditional frame makeup goes out of the window when considering articulated locomotives. These generally employ power bogies, completely self-contained wheel sets with their own cylinders and motion. On a Mallet locomotive the rear power bogie is attached to the boiler and cab in the traditional fashion but the front is pivoted at its rear end to enable the engine to go round sharp curves on the line. Steam is admitted to the cylinders through a flexible pipe.

The Fairlie type takes this concept a stage further. On a single Fairlie, the boiler, cab and tanks are carried on a cradle under which is slung the articulated power bogie. The famed double Fairlie, as seen on the Ffestiniog Railway, uses two power bogies pivoted in the centre of the loco under the cab from which the boiler projects in both directions with separate water spaces and smokeboxes, these giving the impression of two locomotives placed back to back.

The Meyer also uses two power bogies, but under a conventional single boiler/firebox arrangement. The disadvantage of this design is that the rear power bogie

normally sits directly under the firebox, limiting the size of the box. The UK firm of Kitson improved this concept with a design that moved the rear power bogies further back, allowing the firebox to sit between the two. *Monarch,* the last narrow-gauge steam locomotive built for UK industrial use in 1953, was a Kitson-Meyer design. At a glance, Meyer locomotives are sometimes confused with Mallets but the quickest way to tell them apart is that the Mallet cylinders all face forward, whereas those on the Meyer face into each other in the centre, the front power bogie effectively being mounted backwards.

Then there is the equally iconic Garratt, built mainly by Beyer, Peacock & Co of Manchester and which found particular favour in South Africa. In these immensely powerful locomotives, the power bogies are carried under a pair of front and rear tenders. The boiler is carried on a cradle between these tenders with daylight underneath. In the UK, 2ft-gauge Garratts can be seen today working almost daily on the reopened Welsh Highland Railway in Snowdonia. These engines were brought to North Wales from their previous life on South African lines.

RIGHT Two of the main driving wheel sets from Britain's most famous locomotive, Gresley A3 Pacific 4-6-2 *Flying Scotsman*, then undergoing overhaul at the National Railway Museum in York. Note the crank for the inside part of the valve gear, and the balance weights on the wheels.

The wheels

Locomotive wheels can be very large items indeed and, as we have already seen, their size gives a clue to the locomotive's intended purpose. Large coupled wheels, lesser in number, are used for locomotives expected to run at high speed over long distances. The hauling of heavy freight trains at a slower speed favours more wheels of smaller diameter, thus providing a bigger 'footprint' and therefore more grip on the rail.

BELOW Various methods of affixing a locomotive tyre to its wheel.

Flying Scotsman, considered by many to be the 'most famous express loco of all', uses six

driving wheels of 6ft 8in (2,003mm) diameter, while the BR Standard 9F class, the last type built for British Railways and designed for heavy freight haulage, had ten driving wheels of 5ft (1,524mm) diameter.

Taking this concept to the extreme were the single-wheel passenger locos of the late 19th century, which had a pair of driving wheels of 8ft or more in diameter.

Early locomotive wheels were made of cast iron, but these were superseded by cast steel wheels. All steam locomotive wheels have tyres, which are cast steel rings of around 2in (50mm)

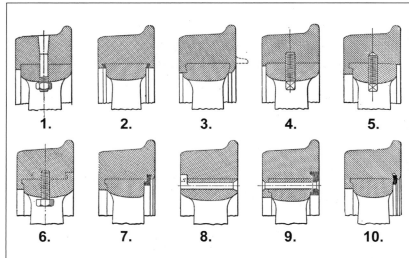

1.   **2.**   **3.**   **4.**   **5.**

6.   **7.**   **8.**   **9.**   **10.**

1   An early, tapered bolt securing a shrunk-on tyre.
2   A recessed lip held in place with molten zinc.
3   A hammered-over flange, which was not popular as removing it destroyed the tyre.
4, 5 and 6   These views show various screw or stud fastenings securing a shrunk-on tyre.
7   Shows a continuous steel retaining ring sprung into a groove in the tyre.
8   Rivets are used to engage in slots in the rim and tyre.
9   The retaining ring is riveted on to the rim and the tyre.
10 A tapered retaining ring is used, hammered down in certain sections to prevent it turning.

LEFT A set of wheels from an outside-framed narrow gauge locomotive, showing the separate cranks. The furthest set, the centre wheels, are flangeless to aid the traversing of sharp curves.

thickness that fit around the wheel. Their role is to add extra strength and to allow worn examples to be replaced without scrapping the entire wheel. The tyre takes all the stresses through contact with the rail.

The inner rim of the tyre is made fractionally smaller in diameter than the wheel it is being designed for and is then fitted by heating. As the tyre cools it shrinks and grips the wheel. This is sufficient for the smaller leading or trailing wheels, but the forces acting through the driving wheels require them to be more firmly secured to prevent the tyre slipping on the wheel. This can be exacerbated by the heat generated when the brakes are applied, or when the wheels slip under heavy load or on greasy rails. Tyres were initially fixed to wheels by studs or rivets, but later locomotives used a Gibson ring. This is a large circlet fitting in a groove mounted on the inner surface of the tyre. A development of this was a double-lipped ring which fits within the tyre and is then completely surrounded by it during the heating process when fitting to the wheel.

Driving wheels are traditionally of a spoked design with up to 20 or more spokes radiating from the wheel centre. However, some smaller and narrow-gauge locomotives use cast plate wheels and these are also commonly used for smaller wheels in the leading or trailing trucks.

The centre hub of the wheel, through which the axle passes, is typically pear shaped on an inside-frame locomotive forming the crank at the end of which a pin is inserted, and upon which the connecting and coupling rods are hung. On outside-frame locomotives the crank is a component in its own right, attached directly to the axle which extends outwards from the wheels through the frames.

To compensate for this significant weight running off-centre, the wheels have balance weights cast into the inner surface of the rim. The main driving wheel, which has the end of the connecting rod on its crank pin as well as the coupling rod, carries a significantly larger balance weight than the other coupled wheels.

All but the smallest locomotives have as part of their running gear additional trucks mounted ahead and/or behind the coupled wheels, carrying smaller wheels which are not coupled together and not driven. Their purpose is simply to spread the weight of the locomotive over a greater number of contact points, therefore reducing the weight pressure on the track. Early locomotive designers dealt with increasing weight by simply increasing the number of coupled wheels, but eventually the fixed wheelbase of the locomotive reached a point where it was too long to negotiate the curves in the track.

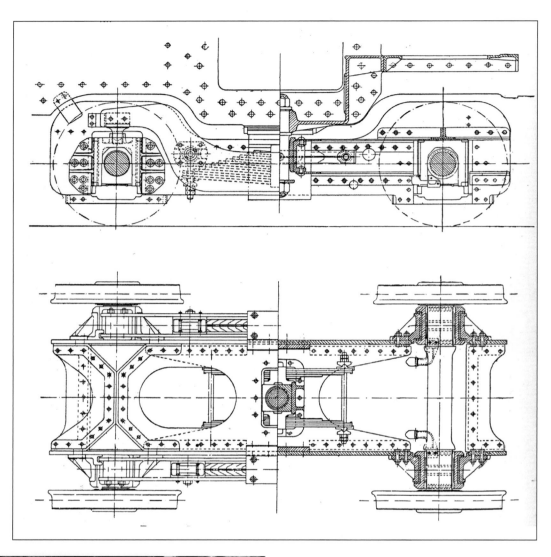

BELOW A two-wheel rear, or trailing pony truck.

Some locomotives have overcome this problem in the simplest way, by having a pair of flangeless coupled axles, usually at the centre, as on the British Railways Standard 9F class 2-10-0, which also had leading and trailing coupled wheels of reduced depth allowing a little more side play on curves.

A more complex solution, particularly outside the UK, involved the fitting of articulated axles on the front and rear axles, a popular version being the Klein-Lindner in which the axle was separate to the wheels, having a ball at its centre which connected to a surround carrying the wheels.

The most simple solution to the weight-versus-curvature issue, used extensively across steam locomotive design, was the creation of bogie and pony trucks. These are simply steel frames carrying four or two wheels respectively, the truck pivoting about a point on a stretcher mounted on the frames. These trucks are independently sprung, with the wheels running in axleboxes, just like in the larger coupled wheels.

The cab

A vital component of the loco 'chassis' is of course the accommodation for its two-person crew – the cab. It is here that all the controls necessary for driving the locomotive are mounted, together with some creature comforts for the driver and fireman. In the earliest days of locomotives, comfort appeared to be the last thing on the mind of the designers, with the only protection for the crew being a short weatherboard mounted in front of them. There was a view that giving them anything more would have been regarded with hostility as enginemen were portrayed as tough characters!

Cabs were, however, soon improved to the point where the crew's place of work became effectively a large steel box, both to protect them and the increasing number of polished brass fittings created to control the locomotive. Yet only on tank locomotives were cabs generally enclosed on all four sides, tender locomotives being open at the back, both to allow the fireman unimpeded access to the coal stocks and to give him plenty of room to swing his shovel and project coal to the front of the long firebox. Most locomotives were also built with partly open sides for access to the footplate, with cab doors more common only outside the UK. Crewing a locomotive in winter was not for the feint-hearted.

Cab design follows broadly similar principles across various types of locomotives with one major variation – which side the driver and fireman occupy. On by far the majority of locomotives the driver sits on the left, the fireman (on the few occasions when he is able to sit) on the right. However, some designs, notably on the Great Western Railway, reversed the practice with a right-hand driver's position, which is also the preferred layout on most narrow-gauge locomotives.

It is vital for both crew to have adequate vision ahead, but this was not easy to achieve considering they were placed up to 40ft (12m) behind the front of the locomotive. Opening

windows are built into the front of the cab (and the rear if the locomotive has one). Most of these are circular and are known as spectacles, the front of the cab dubbed the spectacle plate.

Some locomotives also have sliding side windows but the majority are unglazed, making it easy for the driver and fireman to lean out to get their view ahead.

The spectacle plate or cab front is effectively mounted around the rear of the locomotive firebox and on smaller locomotives, particularly narrow-gauge types, the firebox projects into the cab with many of the controls mounted on it. At the base of the firebox backhead is of course the firehole with its doors.

Naturally, the cab is arranged to site the controls required by each member of the crew closest to them, although in some cases they are

ABOVE The cab of a South Eastern & Chatham Railway O1 class 0-6-0, dating from 1896.

The cab of an LNER Gresley
A4 class locomotive

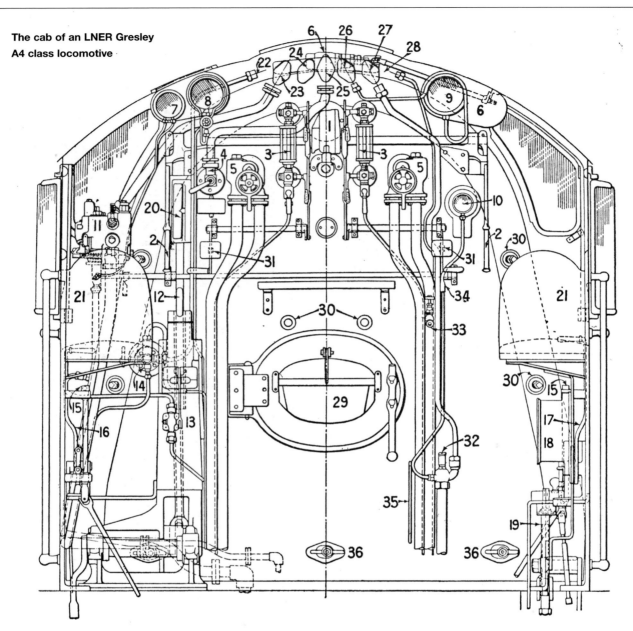

1	Regulator stuffing box.	13	Reversing gear clutch lock.	25	Blower stop valve.
2	Regulator handles.	14	Steam sand valve.	26	Pressure gauge stop valve.
3	Water gauges.	15	Injector water control.	27	Carriage-heating stop valve.
4	Blower valve.	16	Sanding lever.	28	Mechanical lubricator warming valve.
5	Combined steam and delivery valves.	17	Cylinder drain cock lever.	29	Firehole door.
6	Stop valve for steam stand.	18	Speed recorder.	30	Washout plugs.
7	Duplex vacuum gauge.	19	Dropping grate screw.	31	Remote control for water gauge cocks.
8	Steamchest pressure gauge.	20	Cut-off indicator.	32	Carriage-heating safety valve.
9	Boiler pressure gauge.	21	Driver's and fireman's seats.	33	Coal watering cock.
10	Carriage steam heating pressure gauge.	22	Steam sand supply valve.	34	Whistle.
11	Vacuum ejector.	23	Ejector steam stop valve.	35	Damper rod.
12	Reversing screw handle.	24	Blanked off.	36	Handholes.

The cab of a GWR 'King' class 4-6-0 locomotive.

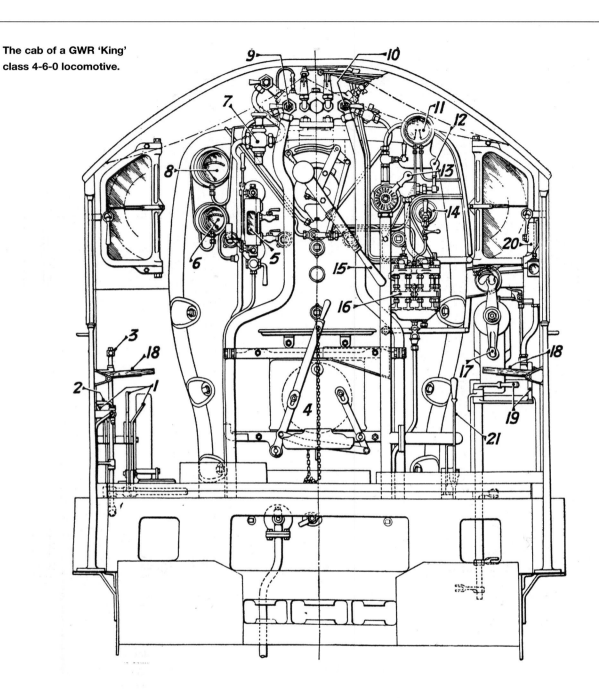

1   Damper controls.
2   Coal-watering cock.
3   Exhaust injector control.
4   Firehole doors.
5   Water gauge.
6   Steam heating pressure gauge.
7   Steam heating valve.
8   Boiler steam pressure gauge.

9   Exhaust injector live steam valve.
10 Righthand injector live steam valve.
11 Vacuum gauge.
12 Ejector steam valve.
13 Ejector air valve.
14 Blower valve.
15 Regulator handle.

16 Lubricator.
17 Reversing handle.
18 Tip-up seats for driver (right) and
     fireman (left).
19 Sanding gear levers.
20 Audible signalling apparatus.
21 Cylinder cock lever.

repeated. The Gresley Pacifics of the London & North Eastern Railway, for example, had vertical regulator handles on both sides of the cab. The two most vital instruments – the steam pressure gauge and the water gauge – will usually be placed high in the cab where both members of the crew can see them easily, although, as we will see later, they are primarily the fireman's responsibility. However, the driver needs to know the condition of his engine and what is available to him by looking at these gauges.

The fireman will have close to hand the controls for the ash pan damper doors and the steam and water valves for the injectors, although the injector controls can sometimes be found on both sides of the cab. Controls for carriage steam heating are also normally placed close to the fireman.

The driver usually has the regulator (effectively the accelerator) close to hand, together with the reverser (the 'gear-lever', which can be of lever or screw type – levers

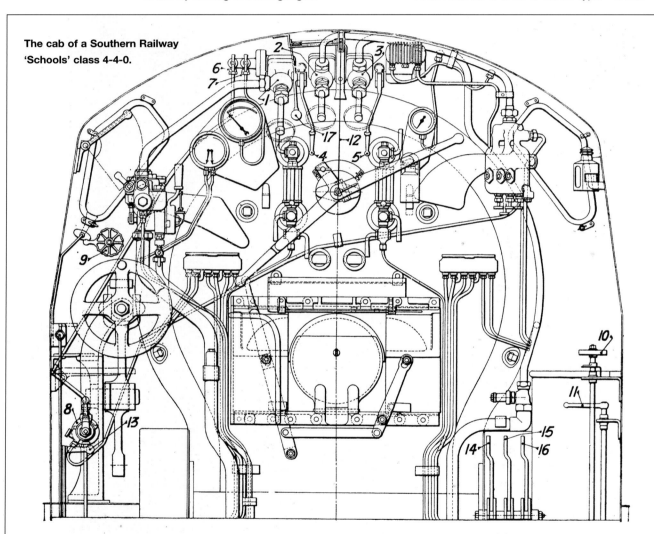

The cab of a Southern Railway 'Schools' class 4-4-0.

1   Vacuum ejector steam valve.
2   Sight-feed lubricator steam valve.
3   Train heating steam valve.
4   Live steam injector steam valve lever.
5   Exhaust injector steam valve lever.
6   Steam to clutch valve.
7   Steam to pressure gauge.
8   Reversing shaft clutch valve.
9   Blower valve handwheel.
10 Water regulator for exhaust injector.
11 Feed cock spindle.
12 Whistle wire.
13 Cylinder drain cocks lever.
14 Front damper lever.
15 Sanding valves lever.
16 Back damper lever.
17 Whistle lever.

RIGHT Smaller, but the principles are the same. This is the cab of a 12¼in-gauge miniature locomotive, based on the 2ft gauge locos of the Indian Darjeeling Railway, and running on the Fairbourne Railway.

are more common on smaller locomotives), the cylinder drain cock lever, and the various controls for the brake system, including the vacuum or air-brake gauge and the ejector controls. We will look at all these controls more closely in the sections on firing and driving.

`The blower is normally placed closer to the driver although it is extensively used by the fireman to encourage or discourage the rate of the fire, and to keep smoke from drifting low, for example over station platforms.

That is standard-gauge practice, but on the narrow gauge the rules tend to be bent a bit in order to make the much smaller cabs a practical working environment for the crew. For example, the two Beyer, Peacock 0-6-0Ts built in 1902 for the author's line, the Welshpool & Llanfair, have both the reversing lever and drain cock controls on the fireman's side, while the injector controls are placed on the cab sides. If the driver is busy and the fireman wants the driver's side injector on, then he/she must dive between the driver's legs!

The 'fuel tank'

Steam locomotives of course need feeding, and for the majority that means a supply of water and coal. Some are oil-fired, some even wood-fired, but these are much rarer compared with coal-fired locos. This requirement for on-board fuel produces one of the most basic differentiating factors between various types of locomotive – whether they are tank or tender engines.

The tender, effectively a wagon usually running on between four and eight wheels, is attached directly to the loco behind the cab,

RIGHT The tender on an Ivatt 2-6-0 No. 46443 on the Severn Valley Railway. The coal is filled in the front section, the water is topped up through the filler at rear, behind the coal bunker.

LEFT This GWR 2-6-2 Prairie tank locomotive, running on the Severn Valley Railway, uses a rear coal bunker, here looking somewhat empty.

BELOW LEFT Former Great Western 2-6-2 Prairie tank No. 5164, based on the Severn Valley Railway, is a prime example of a side tank locomotive.

and is there simply to carry the fuel. On top of the tender frame is a large tank, which is split diagonally, the rear portion carrying water and the front coal. The plate running from the top rear of the tank down to the cab floor helps force the coal down to where the fireman can pick it up on his shovel.

Locomotives without tenders carry their coal in a bunker, effectively a large area, usually at the rear of the cab, open at the top for filling with coal and with a door at its base from which the fireman fills his shovel. Additional, or alternative, storage areas can be employed at the front side of the cab, often in compartments at the rear of side tanks, particularly on small narrow-gauge locos.

Locomotives of this type carry their water in tanks attached to the frames, and are known as tank engines for this reason. However, they can be further distinguished by the type of tanks fitted. Side tanks, as their name suggests, are fitted atop the footplates on either side of the boiler. Both have their own fillers with a pipe running between them so both tanks can be filled from either filler.

RIGHT Great Western 0-6-0PT No. 5764, seen on the Severn Valley Railway, is a pannier tank type.

RIGHT Former Lancashire & Yorkshire Railway 0-4-0ST 'Pug' No. 51241, seen on the East Lancashire Railway, is a typical example of a saddle tank locomotive. *(Eddie Bellass)*

Pannier tanks, used extensively on the Great Western Railway, are similar to side tanks, except that the two tanks are effectively hung from either side of the boiler like the panniers on a horse. Continuing the equestrian theme, the saddle tank is a single tank which fits around the top half of the boiler. Finally, there is the well tank, in which the water is carried in a tank fitted in the space between the main frames.

Sliding and stopping

Before moving on to the actual business of firing and driving a steam locomotive, we should look briefly at two essential elements not covered so far. These are lubrication and braking, and they will feature with further detail in the next sections.

Lubrication

Whatever the type of locomotive, its make-up includes a great many metal parts moving in contact with other metal parts, so adequate lubrication between those components is essential. In the case of parts such as axles, rods and the like, moving in surroundings not affected by steam or extreme heat, lubrication by drip-feed is the norm. The surface is lubricated either through a pad or directly, fed from an oil reservoir above, usually by means of wicks on wires known as worsted trimmings. Looking after these and topping up the reservoirs are among the duties of the driver as we shall see later.

Where internal surfaces affected by steam or hot water must be lubricated there are two popular forms: the hydrostatic or 'sight-feed' lubricator, and the mechanical lubricator. Both can be employed to lubricate cylinders, valves and pistons – in other words areas under pressure – and use a very thick oil to cope with the presence of steam.

The sight-feed lubricator, common on Great Western engines, was a development of the

LEFT AND BELOW Two examples of hand-replenished oil reservoirs. A worsted trimming can be seen in the one below.

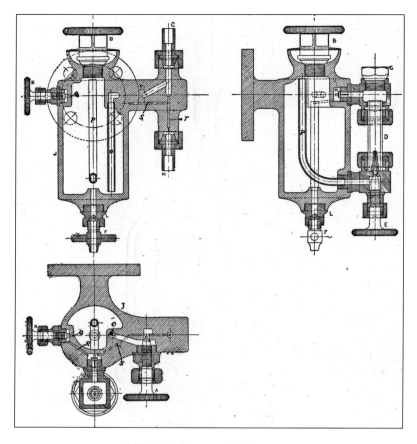

ABOVE **A diagram of a Wakefield sight-feed lubricator.**

BELOW **This diagram depicts a Wakefield mechanical lubricator.**

BELOW RIGHT **A mechanical lubricator as fitted to a standard-gauge locomotive and driven from the motion.**

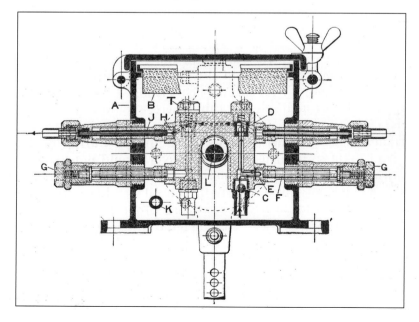

earliest displacement lubricators introduced by John Ramsbottom in 1860. Steam entered a container of oil, condensed to water and fell to the bottom of the chamber, pushing up the oil into the delivery and then the steam pipes, where it was atomised and passed to the cylinders. The sight-feed added a glass to the delivery pipe, mounted in the cab so that the driver could observe the flow rate. Later, the design was developed to more sophisticated lubricators, although still using the same basic principle. The most popular were manufactured by C.C. Wakefield & Co.

While, in such lubricators, steam pressure propels the oil, the mechanical lubricator is directly driven by the motion, and can also be as effectively used to lubricate axle boxes and the like as it can the cylinders. A major advantage of the mechanical lubricator is that it only starts working when the loco starts moving, hence not wasting oil, but continues to work at all times the loco is moving, including when it is coasting and none of the steam that would be required to operate a hydrostatic lubricator is being sent to the cylinders.

Mechanical lubricators are easy to spot, comprising a box mounted on the running plate and with a ratchet on the side joined by a rod to part of the motion, often the crosshead. This drives a series of pumps inside the lubricator itself, immersed in the oil, forcing the lubricant along the delivery pipe.

Brakes

Stopping your locomotive, and a train perhaps weighing 200 tonnes or more, is of course vital, and various methods are employed. The brakes themselves are a basic design, consisting of large blocks made from cast iron and shaped to the outside diameter of the driving wheel. Each block is linked to the others and operating the linkage brings them into contact with the wheels, creating friction, and stopping the loco.

The simplest way to operate the linkage is the handbrake, effectively a handle or wheel on the footplate which operates a screw connected to the brake linkage running to the coupled wheels, pulling on the brakes (turned clockwise) or taking them off (anti-clockwise). Like the handbrake on a car, it is really only used on a loco that has already stopped to prevent it from moving.

The majority of locomotives are fitted with a steam brake. The driver operates a lever in the cab to admit steam (taken from the boiler) into a cylinder, forcing a piston along the cylinder to operate the linkage running to the brake blocks. Locomotives can also be fitted with vacuum or air brakes.

The two major methods of braking a train

LEFT A cast-iron brake block acting on the driving wheel of a locomotive.

are the vacuum brake and the air brake. An Act of Parliament of 1889 following a fatal railway accident at Abbots Ripton declared that all passenger trains must have continuous brakes acting on every wheel of the train. Goods trains, however, can use mechanical brakes working independently on each wagon by a lever on the wagon which is secured by a pin placed through a hole. This is known as 'unfitted' stock.

Before descending a steep gradient, such

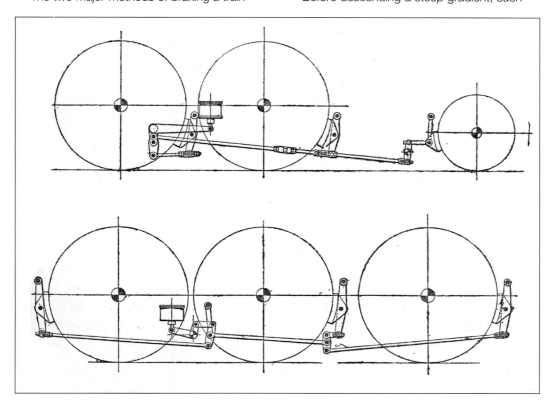

LEFT A diagram showing how the brakes are applied to the wheels of a locomotive.

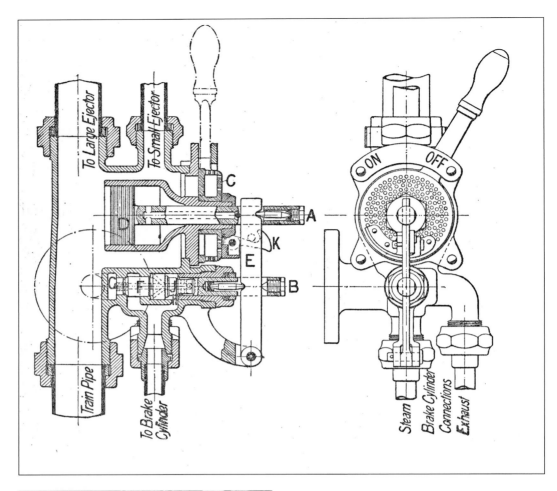

RIGHT A diagram of a driver's vacuum brake control.

To Large Ejector

To Small Ejector

ON OFF

C

D

A

K

E

B

G F

Train Pipe

To Brake Cylinder

Steam

Brake Cylinder Connections

Exhaust

RIGHT The driver's brake control as seen in the cab of a narrow-gauge locomotive.

trains must stop while a member of the crew – often the guard – 'pins down the brakes' by pushing down the levers, putting the brakes partly on and securing them in this state so that the wheels drag on the hill, allowing far easier braking control from the locomotive. It is important not to pin the brakes on too hard of course as this would lead to locked wheels and flat spots worn on their tyres.

In a vacuum-brake setup all the vehicles of the train (including the locomotive) are joined by flexible pipes. Each vehicle has a cylinder on it in which is created a vacuum, keeping the brakes off. This vacuum is created by the driver operating a device known as an ejector, which extracts the air from the system and maintains the vacuum. The ejector is operated from the cab and can be mounted in there, although it is often attached to the smokebox or on the side of the loco close to the footplate.

The ejector works in a similar way to the injector – steam is admitted into it and through a cone where it is combined with the air in the brake pipes. The cone forces the steam to increase in velocity, creating a vacuum which draws the air out of the brake pipes and through a pipe to the base of the chimney, where it is exhausted.

When the vacuum is destroyed by letting air into the system, either by the driver operating the brake or a leak occurring – for example two vacuum pipes separating – the brakes are applied. The major advantage of this of course is that should a train become divided for any reason, the brakes will automatically come on.

Air brakes work in similar fashion to vacuum brakes in that each vehicle in the train is connected by pipes. Compressed air in the pipes, created by a compressor mounted on the loco, operates a cylinder on each vehicle that brings the brakes into use. Air brakes pre-dated vacuum brakes but early versions had a major disadvantage in that if the 'circuit' was broken and the air pressure lost, the brakes would come off rather than on.

American George Westinghouse, credited with inventing the air brake in 1869, came up with a far more effective system three years later which, by means of a triple valve set-up, uses a reduction of air pressure in the system to apply the train's brakes, rather than the other way round.

In the Westinghouse system each vehicle in the train has its own reservoir. If the pressure in the train pipes falls, either by the driver or guard operating the brake or a break in the pipe, the triple valve is moved into a position where air is admitted from the reservoir, pushing the pistons that operate the brake linkage and stopping the train. The air compressor itself comprises a pair of vertically mounted cylinders with a piston moving between them, producing a very distinctive sound, and is usually mounted on the exterior of the locomotive, the most obvious location being on the side of the smokebox.

These are the basics of the steam locomotive, enough for you to demonstrate to the footplate crew undertaking your training that you are not a complete novice. You will learn a great deal more about everything we've outlined above as you progress in your footplate career. So – onto the footplate we go...

ABOVE In this view of a narrow-gauge locomotive on the Welsh Highland Heritage Railway, the air brake pump can be seen mounted on the side of the smokebox.

LEFT The Westinghouse brake pump on a former Great Eastern Railway-design 0-6-2T. *(Eddie Bellass)*

Chapter Three

Stepping on to the footplate

Back in the days when the steam locomotive ruled the railways the footplate was a place of strict hierarchy, and a new recruit embarked on a very long-term career. It would be several months before he was allowed to wield a shovel under the eye of a fireman, and training as a driver was something that only happened after several years of proving that one was a highly competent fireman.

OPPOSITE Becoming a member of a footplate crew is a long process that requires dedication, and essentially, the ability to work as part of a two-man team. Here, a crew is seen preparing the 1954-built Peckett 0-6-0ST *Mardy Monster* at the Elsecar Steam Railway in South Yorkshire.

In today's world of course, steam locomotive driving is no longer generally a career, and at any number of heritage railways you can put down your money and enjoy a day at the regulator of a locomotive under the watchful eye of an experienced driver. But in reality this is only playing, and if you seriously want to become a steam loco driver, you will still need to commit to a goal that initially looks distant. It might not be as far ahead as in the real days of steam, as no-one today has such time available to spend on what is generally a hobby, but it will still be several years down the line.

In those old days of steam the career footplateman started as a cleaner, and there was even a ladder to climb here, progressing from the dirtier, hidden parts of the locomotive to the more visible components. Last of all was the platework viewed by the public, and indeed, progressing from humble shunting engines to the elite passenger-hauling locomotives.

Along the way the recruit learnt all about how a locomotive works, as has been outlined in the first part of this book. This knowledge served him well when he stepped on to the fireman's side of the footplate. Once on that hallowed chequer plate he again moved up the locomotive ladder, from shunting locomotives to goods, passenger, and if he did well, to express passenger engines. Only then was he ready

to start training as a driver, and again to begin climbing yet another ladder.

Several heritage railways today still use the cleaner-fireman-driver system, although of course, with most candidates treating such activities as a leisure-time pursuit the timescales have been somewhat compressed. However, if one has hopes of going 'all the way' to driver the process still requires a long-term commitment. On the Llangollen standard-gauge line for example, one is expected to volunteer for some months in the workshop department before being invited to join the footplate department as a cleaner. The workshop effort is expected to continue alongside footplate training too.

Another prime example is the West Somerset Railway, which at more than 20 miles is Britain's longest standard-gauge heritage line, and which uses a very traditional training method not far removed from British Railways' days. Those with an eye on the footplate first sign up to be a cleaner, which involves attending a number of meetings held every other Saturday for all-day cleaning sessions on locomotives. Once a month on Saturday afternoons firing school is held, not on the locomotive but in a classroom teaching theory, with exams included! Four days spent cleaning then qualify the recruit for a 'Footplate Knowledge Trip', where he can start learning the

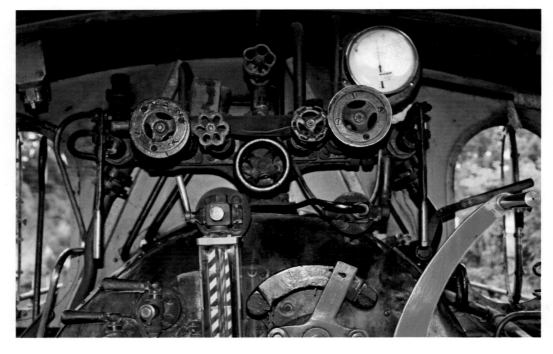

RIGHT A challenge faced by some of today's footplate crews that their forebears did not have is the potential variety of different cab layouts on offer – standard gauge, narrow gauge or miniature, British or globally sourced. This is the upper cab layout of a former Romanian forestry locomotive, with the blower in the centre, the injector steam valves either side, and the injector water valves operated by levers just outside them.

techniques through practising them under the eyes of an experienced driver and fireman.

Assuming these sessions go well, both on the footplate and in the classroom, the cleaner will eventually take exams on the practical and technical aspects they have learnt, and the essential rules test. If they pass these, they become a passed cleaner, which allows them to fire a locomotive when asked to. Following a satisfactory two years at this level a further exam takes place to qualify them as a fireman.

As a fireman the volunteer will learn all aspects of life on the footplate, and again satisfactory completion of these duties, and equally importantly his or her attitude to the work, might see them eventually selected to train as a driver. Again, a number of training turns are followed by exams and for successful candidates a promotion to passed fireman. This is a fireman who is qualified to drive a locomotive when needed, and yes, a number of sessions at this grade will be needed before there is any hope of selection and promotion to the ultimate goal of driver.

This might sound daunting, but it is with good reason. Steam locomotives are not toys, and must be treated with great respect. Intensive training that takes a long period is essential to ensure the safety of one's self, one's crew and the train, to prove to those conducting the training that the candidate 'has what it takes'. Of course, constantly practising the correct techniques is also vital to avoid damaging what in most cases are historic and irreplaceable artefacts.

Not all lines have such a drawn-out training process – particularly those on the narrow gauge. This is not through any lack of consideration for the correct techniques, but in fact accurately reflects history. Most narrow-gauge lines were originally run by small companies where, for example, there were no cleaners, the driver and fireman being responsible for the cleanliness and, in fact, every aspect often including maintenance, of the locomotive they were crewing. So today, such lines may have a shorter training ladder, the first rung being trainee fireman, with the cleaning and learning process incorporated into such training, but the procedure is just as intensive and requires no less effort on the part of the candidate.

On the Welshpool & Llanfair the author was

allowed just a few goes with the shovel on his very first training turn. On average, passing out as a fireman on this line can take around two seasons, but there is still no rapid path to the other side of the footplate. You might be a qualified fireman for at least five years before any possibility of being invited to train as a driver, an invitation that is by no means certain to be offered.

One further aspect worth stating at this point is that this is by no means a male-only vocation. In fact, on today's heritage railway scene there are a great many female enthusiasts working in all departments, very much including the footplate. We refer to the 'fireman' as the phrase remains a traditional railway expression, and we refer to 'he' doing this and that. But in reality plenty of firemen, and drivers, are women, and many of the 'hes' are 'shes' – it is a vocation for all!

ABOVE This is by no means a male-only hobby. On many of today's heritage railways there are a number of female volunteers on both sides of the footplate.

ABOVE As a fireman in particular, you would be expected to shovel much of what is in this locomotive's tender into the firehole during your 'turn', so a degree of physical fitness is essential. Note the pick on the coal pile for breaking up large lumps.
(Geoff Gauntlett)

Before you begin...

So you have signed up to the footplate roster, and have been allocated your first training turn. There are preparations to make before you nervously take your first early morning walk to the locomotive shed.

You should first be sure that you are up to the job in hand. Obviously you should be reasonably fit and healthy as firing a steam locomotive is a very physical activity, especially on the standard gauge, and no easy job on the narrow gauge either. You don't need to be a bodybuilder but you should be aware of the reasonable amount of exertion needed. But equally importantly, you should have a good attitude to yourself and to others. While

the driver is in charge of the locomotive and responsible for it, the driver and fireman work as a team, so it is vital they get on with each other. You will get to know a number of firemen and drivers as your training progresses, and you will grow to like some more than others, but you will need to be able to work with all of them.

The first and foremost priority during your training and your entire footplate career will be safety. You are being let loose with a machine that has the potential to be very dangerous indeed – lethal in fact. While you might be a volunteer on a heritage railway doing all this as a hobby, you will still be bound by exactly the same legislation relating to railways as you would be if driving a High Speed Train on the mainline.

So, safety should always be uppermost

RIGHT Traditional footplate wear for the turn: cotton-based thick trousers with braces, a jacket of the same material, optional heavier jacket which is particularly useful in inclement weather, and headgear. The greasetop is widely used although some prefer a flat cap. The mug of tea is optional, but desirable!

in your mind and it is good from the start to ensure you always allow plenty of time for each task required, doing everything in a methodical way ensures mistakes are less likely. A major point in these modern times, when anywhere near the footplate of a locomotive, even just in the yard, is to *never* wear anything in your ears such as personal stereos, iPods or the like. If a locomotive approaches you from behind you need to be able to hear it coming.

You will require some essential equipment before commencing your training. First, two sets of overalls, but why two? One set will be kept for the 'dirty' parts of the operation, lighting up, ashing-out and the like, while the other will be for the run, when apart from anything else, you will usually be on display to the public.

You can wear boiler-suit type overalls for the public side but most crews prefer a bib-and-brace, as traditionally worn by railwaymen and combined with a jacket, mainly to protect the arms when on the footplate where there are plenty of hot pipes. Don't go and buy from your nearest DIY store as you will need 100 per cent cotton, because garments made from synthetic materials will melt if they come into contact with the very hot temperatures that exist on the footplate. There are specialist suppliers of such overalls, some of which are listed at the back of this book.

You will need heat-resistant gloves. Many railways supply these to their staff but they are easily obtainable and I find they tend to be a disposable item, best chucked away and replaced after a few turns once they get caked in oil and coal dust.

RIGHT Good-quality gloves are essential for protection from the oil, grease and in particular the heat, all of which are part of footplate life. Many heritage lines supply such gloves to their staff.

Proper protective footwear with steel toecaps is also needed. I started off with large boots but so long as they offer full protection to your feet then smaller shoes can be a good idea, especially when climbing on the tanks of narrow-gauge locomotives where there are lots of sticking-out bits of metal in the way.

Headwear is a good idea too, if nothing else, to give your hair some protection from the sooty atmosphere of the footplate. Endlessly debated on enthusiast forums is whether railwaymen should wear the traditional grease-top cap, or a flat cap. The author prefers the flat cap, picked up cheap in a local country store (because again, they can tend to get dirty and need replacement), but so long as your particular railway has no rule on the matter it's up to your personal preference. Please don't wear a baseball cap or similar as it looks wrong, and you will get no thanks from the photographers!

You will also need some kind of footplate bag in which to carry a few essential items such as your rulebook, which most railways require their staff to carry at all times on duty, your grade card (which you receive when you qualify), a torch, particularly for lighting up in the morning as we will see later, and for the same purpose, either a lighter or matches. You might also want to keep some rags in the bag.

I also carry a traditional fob watch. We will see that it is important to keep a close eye on the time when firing, and you can get such watches very cheaply (mine cost around a tenner), yet they add to the image!

When I started on the footplate I soon gained a reputation for how dirty I became, but while this is a naturally dirty environment in places, you should be trying to keep yourself as clean as possible at all times, for health reasons if nothing else. Being too dirty also does not present a very good image to the passengers, the railway's customers, which is why for example, you have a second set of overalls for the muckiest jobs. Every time you leave the staff mess, apply barrier cream to your hands, wash your hands every time you enter the mess, and re-apply the barrier cream before going back to work. Remember the age-old definition of an engineer: someone who washes their hands before going to the toilet as well as after.

Particularly ensure your overalls do not become soaked in oil, as mineral oils include chemicals that can cause a nasty skin condition called dermatitis. Wash your overalls regularly. (A tip is to add soda crystals to the detergent as it helps lift soot and also stops it making a mess of the washing machine and angering the 'domestic authority'.)

If your overalls become too dirty, leave them down at the sheds to be cut up for lighting up rags and get some new ones. Be careful if washing a flat cap as unless you put it back on your head when wet it can shrink and fall off the next time you bend down to pick up a shovel-full of coal.

Cleaning a locomotive

As already noted, in the days of steam on the mainline cleaning was a stage in the footplate crewman's career that lasted a few years. Today, it remains an essential part of locomotive preparation and a specialist task whether you start on the footplate as a pure cleaner or undertake cleaning as part of your firing. Yet while describing below the specific cleaning one carries out to the locomotive, usually at the start of the turn if you are a fireman, you should get into a routine of constantly cleaning behind you to protect both the locomotive and you the crew.

Spilt oil left without mopping-up can easily cause someone to slip. When you've ashed-out the locomotive if you leave some ash on the footplate it will almost certainly end up in the motion, where it will cause lots of expensive damage to carefully polished surfaces. Coal left on the cab floor will form an efficient tripping hazard, especially in the confined space of a narrow-gauge locomotive.

As well as making the locomotive look more attractive to passengers, cleaning forms an essential role in checking it over. Cleaning the grime from the springs, for example, can expose a broken leaf. Different surfaces require different cleaning materials, which the railway will keep in stock, but use them sparingly as they are expensive. First get yourself some rags from the rag bin, these are usually old clothes or bed linen and you should ensure the zips, buttons and the like have been removed to avoid any risk of scratching paintwork.

You will use the cleanest rags for final polishing, and as they get dirty they will be demoted to initial grime removal, and when dirtier still, they will go in a tin of diesel to soak ready for fire lighting. Heritage railways constantly need new rags, so ensure your family keep any old sheets, clothes and the like to go in the rags bin.

Normally, one starts cleaning at the top of the locomotive, quite simply because once lit up the top becomes a not very nice environment for cleaning! Brasswork, such as safety-valve covers, whistles and on some engines chimney caps should be done first as once the fire is lit they will soon get uncomfortably hot and in some cases can spit steaming water. For the same reason cab controls and particularly their pipes should be done early as they soon get hot.

For cleaning brass or copper a good-quality metal polish is absolutely fine, combined with steel wool for stubborn marks. However, if pipework has become tarnished, a more effective solution is needed, usually a fine emery paper and thin oil. This has to be done very carefully to avoid the emery wearing the wall of the pipe, and involves soaking the area in oil, wrapping the emery around it and covering with oil, then pulling it back and forth to remove the dirt in the oil.

Paintwork, such as on the boiler sides, tanks and cab, is possibly the easiest to clean as all you need is a polish, usually car polish. Check first, though, that there are no bits of ash, grit or such like on the paintwork as this will need brushing away to avoid any danger of scratching. If the paintwork is significantly dirty, usually a condition caused by 'priming' which sends dirty water out of the chimney, then it should be washed first using a sponge and hot water, to which a car shampoo or washing up liquid can be added. When applying the polish, wet your cloth first as then the polish will go a lot further. Polish it off with a second cloth.

Some locomotives with matt black platework, such as Continental industrial engines, respond well to being cleaned with a mixture of engine oil and red diesel or paraffin. When rubbed down it gives an attractive finish although it can easily attract dust and dirt particles.

It is equally important to clean below footplate level including the wheels, motion and

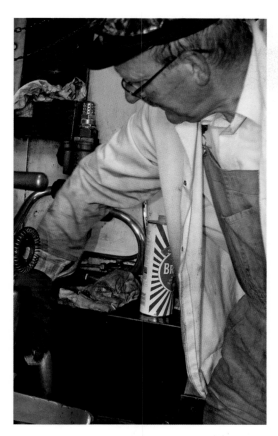

LEFT The first job for cleaning is much of the locomotive's brass work because once the fire is lit such fittings will quickly become too hot to touch. There is no substitute for a quality brass liquid cleaner.

LEFT Polishing paintwork is carried out using car polish. Wetting the cloth with which it is applied helps the polish go a lot further.

frames. These are of course more difficult to get at, but they also get much dirtier due to their location close to the line and all the parts that make the mess, such as the ash pan.

When cleaning down below the secret ingredient is diesel oil. Don't be tempted to use a modern aid such as a steam cleaner or power-washer as this will result in cups full of water in lots of areas that you really don't want it such as in axle boxes and oil reservoirs. As oil floats on water, you won't be able to see the problem, the solving of which is a long job, using an oil syringe to suck out the invading liquid.

Far better is to use diesel, which you apply on the areas to be cleaned using a paintbrush, then wipe off with cotton rags. With a bit of elbow grease this can bring up quite a nice shine on the parts concerned. Such techniques work as well on the unpainted bright steel motion parts as they do on the frames and wheels, which are usually painted. It is not unusual to find rust spots on the motion parts and these need slightly more attention. This is almost exactly the same method as for cleaning tarnished pipes, involving thin oil and emery paper – applying the oil first and then carefully rubbing the area with the emery paper. This will produce a black residue that should be cleaned off immediately and crucially, not allowed to get into the motion where parts rub together. Once this is done a traditional technique is to make up 70/30 mixture of cooking oil and paraffin, which can be applied to the steel parts and helps prevent the rust from returning.

Sometimes parts will be seriously tarnished, but hopefully not too often on a regularly working locomotive. In cases like this, using some powered abrasive cleaning tool might be necessary, but this is never something you as a fireman should undertake until you have been trained to do so.

How it used to be – by Frank Podmore

Today living in Wales, and a volunteer locomotive driver on the Welshpool & Llanfair Light Railway, Frank was a career railwayman in the age of steam, firing locomotives on the Southern Region. In this and the next chapter, he offers a flavour of life on the footplate in those days.

I began as an engine cleaner in July 1953 at Eastleigh shed near Southampton. It was a large depot with around 140 locomotives stabled there in the days before the arrival of diesel and electric stock.

At that time your date of joining became your seniority date and went with you throughout your employment on the railway. So, if a vacancy arose for a passed cleaner your

BELOW Unpainted metal parts can be brought up to standard using diesel and a light abrasive pad to carefully remove tarnished areas.

seniority date would promote you over everyone else who had joined later.

After about six weeks I was promoted to a passed cleaner, having answered questions about the rule book and about locomotives, asked by the shed foreman.

At that time cleaners were not allowed on the footplate, but as a passed cleaner you were. There was a 2.10pm shift on a Sunday known as steam-raising. Locomotives were lit up by carrying a 'hod' of live fire from the sand-drying furnace, which was emptied into the firebox and coal from the locomotive tender put on to it.

The job of the passed cleaner was to go around a number of locomotives, keeping the fire alight, building up the steam pressure and the water ready for the locomotive crew when they signed on duty. This also involved using the injectors on the locomotive.

As a passed cleaner you could be called upon to go as a fireman on the running line. I was 16½ when I had my first trip as a fireman, a football special from Eastleigh to Southampton Central and back, about seven miles each way on T9 class locomotive No. 30120, today preserved on the Bodmin & Wenford Railway. I was also sent down to Southampton Docks and Bournemouth as a fireman.

Your seniority date carried you onwards and upwards. My first 'link' as a proper fireman was on the carriage shunting station pilot locomotive. Then followed goods shunting and the 'ash pan gang' – moving locomotives down to the pit for coal and water and raking out of the ash pan.

The seniority date promoted you through all the links to mainline, whether you were good, bad or indifferent at the job. If you were a bad fireman, however, reports from drivers to the running shed foreman usually resulted in a summons to his office and being told in no uncertain manner to pull one's finger out or else. It usually worked.

A senior fireman who was looking to be promoted to passed fireman had to take a train out to a destination with the locomotive crew inspector in attendance, just like a car driving test.

Cleaning a locomotive in the 1950s involved the use of rags known as 'Rusties' which were issued by the stores. One rag would wipe away the surface grime, the second rag was dropped into a bucket with oil in it and wiped onto the surface, and it was then wiped off with a third rag. We used no gloves in those days.

If a locomotive required to be specially prepared, for a Royal Train perhaps or a 'Dignitary Special', a light oil was used on the paintwork and polished off. After such treatment, which could take two days' work and extended to white tyres on the wheels, the locomotive looked immaculate.

In those days a young fireman was given advice by the driver and learnt by experience and mistakes.

BELOW Steam-age loco crew still on the footplate today, Frank Podmore (right) with his fireman John Winsper are attired in traditional bibs, braces and jackets, with grease-top hats, ready for a turn on the Welshpool & Llanfair Light Railway.

Chapter Four

Firing a steam locomotive

When I first 'passed out' as a fireman I was, of course, delighted and wasted no time at all telling family and friends that I was now a qualified steam locomotive fireman. The most frequent reply I had, was: 'Oh, you are the one that shovels the coal into the hole'. It is a misconception, but a widely held one, that shovelling coal is all that the fireman is there for, a physical but not exactly skilled job.

OPPOSITE As a fireman you will be working in the hallowed environment of a steam loco shed, from which many railways today, deny access to casual visitors, citing 'health & safety'. While this photo was taken some years ago at the Severn Valley Railway's Bridgnorth shed, the environment remains little changed.

ABOVE Early morning in the shed, with a locomotive ready to be lit up. Although this is a narrow-gauge locomotive the procedure is similar across today's heritage railways.

In fact, as we will learn shortly, the fireman's job is a complex and wide-ranging role that requires knowledge, skill, and multi-tasking. On the line, or 'the road' as it is known in railway terminology, firemen are just as essential on the footplate as is the driver. But before we learn what those skills are we have to get our locomotive going, a complex and long-winded process in itself.

The fireman's duties – raising steam

The first step in firing a steam locomotive is of course lighting it up, and this is by no means a simple process and is certainly not like lighting a fire in your living room fireplace. A number of procedures must be carried out, first to ensure the engine is safe to bring to life, and then to avoid suffering the ultimate embarrassment of your carefully made fire going out and having to be started again.

Again, locomotives of different gauges require different techniques, and there will also be varying procedures between individual railway lines. Your footplate training will include close instruction in the way your particular railway 'does it', so rather than simply describe a generic set of procedures, it is probably more informative to look at a case study. In this example it is on the narrow-gauge railway on which I regularly fire myself. Assuming you are preparing an engine for a typical day's work, you will be setting your alarm for a very early call.

Lighting up on the Welshpool & Llanfair Light Railway

On the 2ft 6in gauge Welshpool & Llanfair Light Railway in Mid-Wales there are no cleaners, the lowest 'rank' being trainee fireman. Therefore the fireman carries out the entire lighting-up process themself, or if they are lucky, assisted by a trainee.

Before heading to the shed, the first step is to sign on. This is essential for insurance purposes, and also to check the standing notices in the office for anything new. While most notices are for the driver, dealing with temporary speed restrictions on the line and the like, it is useful for the fireman to know this so he can remind the driver if necessary. The notices will also advise on any potential technical issues with your locomotive that might have been logged by the previous crew, but not yet attended to by the workshop department. Minor faults, which do not impede the locomotive working are often left to a more convenient time, such as at the end of a locomotive's roster period, but it is always useful to know the fault is there.

At this point it is also worth checking that you have your essentials with you including the rule book and grade card which you must carry, your torch and something with which to light up. Some people use long matches but I prefer cheap cigarette lighters, of which you can get several for around a pound at market stalls and pound shops.

Typically, a fireman's duty on the Welshpool line starts three to three and a half hours before the departure of the first train of the day, which is usually around 10am. So one should be unlocking the shed door around 6.30am, but this can vary. The Welshpool line is one of those that does not completely empty its fires at the end of the day, in order to let the engine cool gently and reduce the risk of thermal shocks to the metal parts. If the locomotive is stone cold, say on a Saturday morning when the line is only running at weekends, then lighting it up will take significantly longer than on the Sunday morning when the locomotive will still have the warm remains of the previous day's fire in it. It is worth remembering too, that the W&LLR engines are narrow gauge and a large, standard-gauge locomotive can take eight hours to warm up from cold. If one of these has not been used for a while, a small fire will often be lit in it the previous day and allowed to burn out to begin the warming process.

Climbing on to the footplate you first make three checks: 1. The handbrake is on (the easy way to remember is left is loose, right is tight); 2. The reverser is in mid gear and 3. The cylinder drain cocks are open. This is to ensure that as steam is raised the locomotive doesn't decide to move off by itself.

The next check is to ensure there is water in the boiler. The disposing crew should have left the water gauge closed, to ensure there is no chance of the water in the boiler draining away overnight. Our next step therefore is to open the gauge and then open the drain, closing it again to 'bob' the water level in the glass and obtain a true reading. Individual locomotives vary, but generally

THE WATER GAUGE

The water gauge is possibly the most essential item in the cab as it shows the level of water in the boiler. If the level is too high the locomotive can suffer from priming, which we will study shortly. If the level drops too low, the firebox crown can be exposed, melting the lead in the fusible plugs and sending a shower of steam and water into the firebox, ending the locomotive's work for the day there and then.

By far the most common type of gauge is one that has top and bottom fittings with a pillar of glass tube mounted vertically between them. The level of water in the glass matches that in the boiler. To protect the crew from the dangers of the glass shattering under pressure, it is encased in a gauge frame of thick, toughened glass. The top (steam) and bottom (water) fittings have levers, known as cocks and sometimes connected, allowing you to open and close the gauge. You open it up, and you shut it down. There is also a third cock at the bottom allowing you to drain the glass when the gauge is shut.

It is essential the glass and its frame are clean so that the water level can be viewed easily by both driver and fireman. A fireman must know how to both clean and dismantle and reassemble the gauge as he may need to replace a glass that has shattered on the road. The illustrations on the following two pages portray the procedure for a typical glass although your railway's written information for firemen should give more detail on the particular gauges fitted to your steam fleet. For clarity, the procedure has been illustrated with a training gauge frame, not one mounted on an engine.

Cleaning a gauge glass
This is best done once the early smoke has cleared from the cab following lighting-up, but before the boiler gets too hot.

1 The top and bottom cocks are moved down, shutting off the gauge so as to avoid the danger of it shattering without the protector in place.
2 The water in the gauge is drained by opening the drain cock at the base. Leave this open.
3 The rear plate of the protector is slid out sideways and the rest of the frame removed by slackening a nut, which should only be finger tight, and lifting out. It can then be cleaned, warm water being best for this task.
4 The protector is replaced in the reverse of the removal process, ensuring the nut is only finger tight.
5 The top cock is then opened *slowly*, which will allow steam to blow through the glass, ensuring it is not warmed too suddenly, which runs the risk of shattering the glass.
6 The bottom cock is then opened slowly, allowing water to run through the glass, and finally the drain cock is closed, again slowly, allowing the water to rise and show the level in the boiler. If the gauge has its top and bottom cocks linked, then they are blown through together, but the slowly rule still very much applies.

The testing of water gauges is normally done with about 80psi on the pressure gauge. The top and bottom cocks are closed, and the drain cock opened to drain water from the glass. The top cock is then opened, steam blown through and the cock closed. The same procedure is followed with the bottom water cock. The drain cock is closed and the top and bottom cocks then slowly opened, allowing the water to rise to its original level.

CHANGING A GAUGE GLASS

If you are called upon to do this job it will likely be under pressure, with steam and water blowing everywhere following the failure of the glass, either by cracking or bursting. As in these pictures, many railways have gauge frames mounted for firemen to practice the technique.

You will need gloves or a thick layer of rags to avoid your hands getting burnt. Shut both gauge cocks and then open the drain cock. Having isolated the gauge from the boiler, all three cocks must not now be touched until the replacement is complete.

The gauge glass is held in position by a rubber-tapered washer, a metal 'follower' ring and a lock-nut on the top and bottom. Having removed the protector as described earlier, unscrew the top and bottom nuts, the washers

and the followers, holding the glass in place, together with the top blanking plug. It is important to remember the order they are taken out so they can be reassembled correctly.

Carefully clean out any pieces of broken glass remaining in the fittings. Then it is essential to pass the new glass through the top fitting and then place the fittings on it, ensuring you get them in the right order.

Ensure the glass sits properly in the bottom fitting and extends into the top fitting, but not too far, otherwise it might restrict the inlet from the boiler.

Replace the top blanking plug and tighten it, carefully, finger tight.

Tighten the two gland nuts, again as tight as finger pressure will allow.

Replace the protector, then open the steam and water cocks slowly just as when testing the gauge.

ABOVE A water gauge, open and showing a healthy level: 'three quarters of a glass'. Keeping the glass of the gauge protector and its backplate clean is essential to be able to read the gauge easily.

These pictures show the changing of a gauge glass, using a practice frame for clarity. In the cab, the fireman would be wearing gloves as the conditions would involve hot steam, water and broken glass.

First, close the gauge by moving the top and bottom cocks down, and drain the gauge of water. These three cocks should not now be touched until the replacement is complete.

The top and bottom nuts are slackened and slid down the glass, if this is still present. The top blanking plug is also removed at this point.

After the nut come the follower (visible sitting in the top nut at the base of the picture) and then the rubber seal.

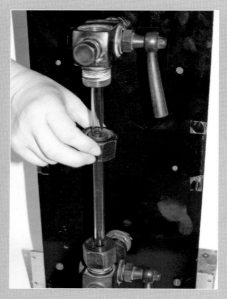

The glass can then be lifted through the blanking plug hole and out of the way.

It is essential to check that the passageways in the top and bottom of the gauge are clear, especially if the glass has shattered as there may be loose shards left behind.

Refitting with a new glass is the reverse of removal. The glass is slid through the blanking hole and then the components fitted to it in the correct order, as shown in the next picture.

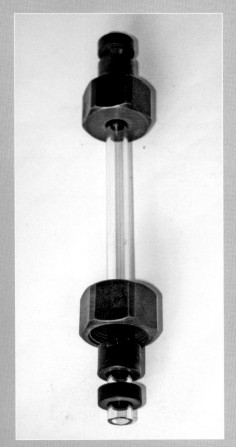

It is essential to get the parts in the right order. From the middle, top and bottom should be placed in the order of nut, follower and rubber seal.

Spare gauge glasses are kept in a box on the footplate, complete with their rubbers. The fireman checks they are there before each turn.

ABOVE To check fusible plugs there really is no substitute for sticking one's head inside the firehole door – carefully, as if the locomotive was used recently it can still be quite warm in there.

RIGHT This is a fusible plug in the crown of the firebox, seen in the centre containing a hole that is filled with lead. Any sign of dampness around this, or on the firebed, is a serious cause for concern and will likely see the locomotive declared a failure.

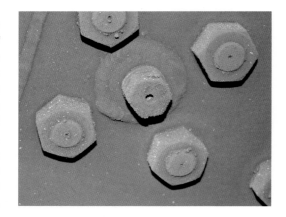

ABOVE The first step in the light-up procedure is to check the water level in the boiler. The water gauge is opened and its level observed, checking by 'bobbing' the level.

BELOW The Welshpool & Llanfair leaves its fires to die naturally so the next-turn fireman will be confronted by the remains. Also notable in this view are a couple of blocked tubes.

BELOW The traditional smokebox uses a central dart which fits in a horizontal slot in a bar running across the inside of the smokebox. To secure the door the dart is rotated through 90 degrees using one of two handles on the outside. The second handle has a screw thread which tightens the door and seals it. Also visible here is the spark arrestor.

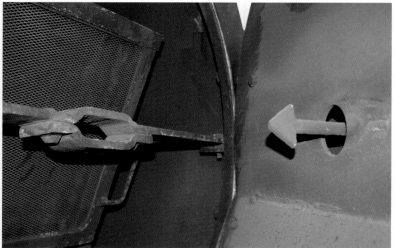

at least a quarter of a glass of water should be present. If the level is lower, then you will likely need to put water into the boiler. This is achieved in different ways depending on the locomotive, but this usually involves connecting a hosepipe to a lance cock fitting on the locomotive. Sometimes you will need to turn a valve on the locomotive to ensure the water goes in.

It is worth remembering, by the way, that the water in the gauge glass will rise a little as the boiler warms up, simply because water expands as it is heated.

With a satisfactory water level the next step is to take the torch and stick one's head in the firebox. You are primarily checking the condition of the fusible plugs, of which there will usually be one or two in the roof of the firebox. If there is any sign of dampness either around the plug or on the ashy remains of the previous day's fire, you will need to fetch your driver immediately, as it most likely indicates that the plug is beginning to leak, in which case the locomotive will not be going anywhere today.

While you are looking in the firebox shine your torch (or alternatively a lead lamp if you have one) around to check on the general

ABOVE LEFT
The smokebox is being checked with particular attention paid to the condition of the spark arrestor and the washout plugs.

ABOVE Use of a fire-iron known as the pricker helps to push the ash through the firebars and into the ash pan for later disposal.

LEFT Some firemen prefer to lift out a firebar in order to drop the ash into the ash pan below more easily.

91

condition of the box, including the seams, the ends of the boiler tubes for any signs that all is not well, and particularly, any evidence of leaks. Potential damage to firebars should also be checked, although if yours is a line that leaves its fires in overnight you will not be able to make this check until the ash and clinker have been removed from the previous fire, as described shortly.

Assuming all looks well you then move to the front end of the locomotive (taking the footplate brush with you), pausing to look into the water tanks. If the level is low, it's worth putting a hosepipe in to fill them while you light up. The chimney cover is removed. Those used on the W&LLR locomotives have long handles on the caps so they can be removed without climbing on the engine.

This is important as company regulations forbid working above footplate level unless two people are present, and the fireman is usually in the shed for at least half-an-hour before his driver, so his movements are restricted unless a trainee is present. If you are lucky, when the driver does arrive he brings a cup of tea with him!

The smokebox door is now unlocked. On most engines this involves two levers, loosening the outer one releases the inner one which is turned through 90 degrees, unlocking its dart, and swinging the door open. However, many Continental engines, of which there are quite a few these days on several UK lines, have a number of dog catches around the door edge which require some dexterity to release.

SPARK ARRESTORS

Spark arrestors are usually held in the smokebox by pins, but the method varies from locomotive to locomotive. On the W&LLR's two original Beyer, Peacock locomotives a large and very heavy metal bar, into which the smokebox door dart fits, has to be lifted clear to release the arrestor. Of course, when you refit the arrestor you again have to lift out the bar, by which time it is rather hot, so gloves are essential!

Finally, when you take the pins out, the worst move is to leave them on the edge of the footplate where they can be knocked off while you are cleaning, and invariably they land somewhere inaccessible. W&LLR locomotives are lit up over an inspection pit and searching for a lost pin in the bottom of this pit early in the morning is not the best way to start the day. (I know, through experience.)

There are further washout plugs in the front end and these are checked with the aid of the torch. Sometimes they are difficult to see, obscured by the blastpipe and spark arrestor, but again, a tell-tale sign of trouble is any evidence of dampness on the floor of the smokebox. If you see damp, *do not* light up – you must get your driver to check.

Assuming all is okay with the plugs, you then check the boiler tube ends are clear of ash, and that ash from the previous working has been cleared out. The disposing crew should have done this job, but you must never assume they have done this without checking.

You now have a look at the general condition of the smokebox, again, for evidence of leaks, or for example, to see if any of the fireclay used to seal around the base of the blastpipe has come loose as this could affect the vacuum sealing of the box and therefore steaming.

At this point, some firemen remove the engine's spark arrestor while lighting up to aid the free flow of air before the fire really gets going. Others leave it in and check it periodically for blinding (ash particles blocking the grille and strangling the airflow). Of course, each check requires opening the smokebox, which can become a tedious task but if you do remove the arrestor it is vital to remember to put it back before you leave the shed. Causing lineside fires will not endear your railway to its neighbours.

Whether the spark arrestor is removed or not the smokebox door needs to be shut tight, or the vacuum will be destroyed and the fire will struggle to come to life. So before you shut it, check the seal and clean around the edge with the footplate brush, removing any stray ash particles to ensure a tight seal. A smokebox door that is drawing air will usually show a blue tinge on its surface, or a whiter patch on the smokebox itself.

In the shed there should be a pile of cut wood ready for lighting-up. You grab a good armful of this, of various sizes, and transfer it to your footplate. You should also be able to find a tin of rags soaked in diesel, although do ensure it is diesel (the smell should give you a clue). Many conscientious firemen, by the way, pop into the shed the night before a footplate turn to check on the stocks of wood and diesel-soaked rags.

On your plug check you would have noticed

whether there is any clinker, fused lumps of ash, on the grate. The amount of clinker is also a good clue to the quality of the coal you will be using. Any clinker found should be lifted out, preferably placed on the fire shovel and disposed of to keep the footplate clean. If the coal is particularly bad the clinker may have glued itself to the firebars and will need chipping off, which is an onerous task.

Taking one of your lumps of wood, you then reach into the back corners of the box (i.e. those nearest you) and under the door, and push any ash forward to the front. On an engine with a traditional grate all the ash in the box is poked through the bars to the ash pan, using a long length of iron bar with its end bent through 90 degrees, which is known as the pricker. Some firemen lift out a firebar and push the ash through, but I prefer the breaking-up method despite the dust it creates as a removed fire bar can be a nightmare to put back.

Of course, if your engine has a rocking grate the process is much less labour-intensive. It is simply a case of operating the lever which tips the grate sections, sending the ash falling into the pan. It is prudent to rock it a couple of times and to check it is fully seated and level when finished. You should also ensure the grate's locking pin has been replaced after the operation as you don't want your fire suddenly dropping into the ash pan while you are out on the trip!

You do not need to be able to eat your dinner off the grate, but you do need to ensure it is clear, especially with no bits of clinker stuck in the essential air space between bars. Ignoring them will cause you troubles later with bad steaming on the road. Stick your head in again and check the back corners, these are often neglected.

If, during your training, you are assigned to 20 different firemen, you will be shown 20 different methods to lay a fire. Some will create neat boxes or 'pyramids' in wood, others will simply chuck in lengths in a sort of criss-cross pattern. Every method works (otherwise their exponents would not be firemen) and over time you will develop your own preferred way of doing it. My method described here is therefore not necessarily the 'right' way, but it works for me.

With a clear grate I first put a layer of coal across the box. This is easy on most of our

LEFT With the grate clear, a layer of coal is put across it, using large lumps with plenty of air space between them.

locomotives which have wide, short grates. The exception is the Romanian 'Resita' 0-8-0T, which has a long, narrow grate, so the fire is generally concentrated on the closer half of it and then spread forward as it gets going. The coal layer should be even, covering the grate with fairly large lumps and nice air space between them, not small dusty bits which can block the flow.

On to this I lay lengths of wood in a loose criss-cross pattern, including some long bits to

LEFT Wood is added on top of the coal. Different firemen have different techniques for the way they lay the wood in the box, the basic theory is, do whatever works best for you.

ABOVE The wood in the firebox. This fireman prefers a criss-cross pattern.

RIGHT A tin of old rags (usually those formerly used for cleaning until they became too dirty), which have been marinating in diesel, should be to hand. These are dropped between and underneath the wood.

LEFT Another diesel-soaked rag is then laid along the shovel and its end lit. The idea is to use this to light the rags already in the firebox, before dropping it in.

BELOW An encouraging sign – the fire is alight. Now it is time to close the door and get on with cleaning while keeping an eye on the fire's progress.

reach right into the corners, but one little trick I add, is to dip both ends of each piece in the tin of diesel before putting it in the box. Using another length of wood I then drop diesel-soaked rags into the gaps between the lengths, preferably so they fall below the level of the wood.

Now for the moment of truth. First, I check that the dampers are open to ensure air gets to the fire from underneath. Then, putting a couple of soaked rags on the shovel, with the one at the front hanging down off the end, I light them. The hanging down length is used to try to light the rags already in the box, and then the rags are slid off the shovel into the box and the doors closed. Job done – for now.

Once the fire is lit it will take a significant time to boil the water in the boiler and create steam, so this time is used effectively in cleaning the engine, as described earlier. However, it is essential to check on the fire's progress regularly, as it is quite easy for it to go out at this stage, especially as there will not yet be enough pressure to use the blower in the smokebox to help draw air up through the fire. What you can use instead is compressed air.

In the running shed at Llanfair we have a supply that connects to a valve on the engine (usually either in the cab or on the side of the smokebox, the method being in the fireman's notes for the engine concerned), and provides a draft for the fire. Once significant pressure shows on the pressure gauge the engine's own blower can be cracked open to take over and the air supply disconnected. Both the air supply and blower have the additional advantage of keeping smoke from blowing back into the cab from the firebox.

If all goes to plan the fire will grow and as a result so will the steam pressure, helped by careful but not over-enthusiastic applications of coal (you don't want a roaring great fire resulting in so much steam pressure that the safety valves blow with an hour still to go to train time).

With around 80–100psi on the clock the driver will likely move the locomotive out of the shed so he can check it over the inspection pit in daylight. Before he does so you must remember to put the spark arrestor back, if taken out during fire lighting. You should also check the water gauges for any potential obstructions in the waterways by blowing them through (as described on page 87).

Testing the gauges is also a reminder to check that certain other items are on the locomotive. Principally these are the replacement gauge glasses and their rubbers, which are usually kept safe in a box, and anything else specific to your line. On the W&LLR we have for many years, carried a red flag, which has been used by the fireman to protect the train at ungated level crossings. At the time of writing, changes to the crossings are seeing this process phased out.

Once outside there are vital duties to carry out, not least checking the injectors to pump water into the boiler. Generally, there are two, and both should be working properly for the locomotive to be fit for service. They are operated by either wheels or levers and the usual procedure is to open the water valve, which will send water gushing out of the overflow by the side of the cab, and then open the steam valve. There should be a brief rush of steam from the overflow and then nothing but a 'singing' sound which you will soon come to recognise as water passes to the boiler. If water or steam continues to come out of the overflow the injector is not picking up and you may need to trim it, adjusting the water valve to make it pick up. We will look at using the injectors in more detail shortly.

The injectors will soon be needed for when the driver blows down the boiler to remove sludge and scale from it, but first he will move the locomotive over the inspection pit to check underneath. While on the pit you should never use the injectors without getting the driver's approval, and you should keep the dampers closed. Scalding or burning your driver with a hot piece of coal down the back of the neck is not a move to ensure a long footplate career.

On our line a boiler blowdown is generally carried out in the morning but many lines do this at the end of the day. The fire needs to be built up carefully to ensure enough pressure is available to fill the boiler before blowdown, and again to refill to a suitable level following the process. During blowdown, which is carried out over a specially designed drain in the track, steam is blown out of the boiler at high

The blowdown can be carried out at the start or the end of the day and is always a dramatic process. Steam is blown out of the boiler at high speed, hopefully taking any sludge and scale with it.

speed, hopefully taking any sludge and scale with it. Typically, the driver blows down 'three quarters of a glass', which means going from a full water gauge to the gauge reading only a quarter, which is why you will need enough pressure to put water back in again afterwards.

From blowdown the locomotive proceeds to the ashpit, where the ash, mainly from the previous day's fire, is raked out to provide plenty of air space under the fire for today's work. When raking out the ash it is a good idea to have someone alongside playing a hose over it to damp down the dust and avoid particles getting on the engine's motion. However, it must be ensured the hose does not point upwards allowing cold water to hit the hot fire grate, where it could cause all sorts of unwanted stresses. On some locos, particularly larger standard-gauge ones, the dumping of ash is a much simpler process as they are fitted with hopper ash pans, which on the simple pull of a lever, dispose of it all in one go. It is also

vital after emptying the ash pan, to ensure any doors are fully closed. Lineside fires can just as easily be started by hot embers escaping from the ash pan as sparks from the firebox.

Finally, the locomotive proceeds to the water column and then to the coal stage, to ensure it is full of fuel for the journey. On the W&LLR this stage of the preparation is normally carried out by the second crew, giving the first crew time to have some breakfast and change into their clean overalls for the 'trip', the first train of the day.

On your particular line you may be filling a saddle tank, a well tank, or even a tender with water, and you might be using a tower or a water crane on the platform. The locomotives

BELOW Ashing out the ash pan on the Welshpool line. This is something that is done at both the start and end of the day, and can also be carried out during the day if the coal is of poor quality. While one crew member rakes, the other has a hose at the ready to damp down the dust to avoid it getting into such areas as the motion.

ABOVE AND ABOVE RIGHT On most railways water is taken either from a crane on the platform, or from a column or tower. Both of these features are on the Gloucestershire Warwickshire Railway.

RIGHT AND BELOW Filling a saddle tank on the Kent & East Sussex Railway, and a tender on the East Lancashire Railway. *(Below: Eddie Bellass)*.

LEFT Watering a side tank locomotive on the Welshpool line. Both fillers are open to monitor the flow.

on the Welshpool & Llanfair are all side tanks, fed from water towers. To fill the tanks one opens both fillers so that as the tanks are filled from one side, the rising level can be monitored on the other side. Before this, however, it will often be necessary to add a water treatment. This helps guard against impurities and scale forming in the boiler and on our line would have been prepared earlier by the driver. Usually, the fireman adds an equal amount before each return trip (i.e. three return trips, one third of the bottle each time), and he does it carefully, using gloves and goggles, as water treatment is a highly toxic liquid. So for example, if filling up alongside a station platform, the treatment would be added to the filler on the opposite tank to the platform.

When the water level gets close to the top of the tank one has to be careful with the filler

as the balance pipe takes water across to the opposite tank, usually at a slower rate than the filler hose, so one has to trickle the water in to allow the other tank to fill. Overflowing the tank is a very bad move. You may be unfortunate enough to soak your driver if he is working below, but more importantly you will fill various oil reservoirs with water, which clearly is not at all good for them.

Coal on the W&LLR locomotives is loaded in buckets that are manhandled on to the footplate and tipped into the bunker. While this is a labour-intensive job, it also provides some measure of fuel consumption by counting the buckets needed to fill the bunker. Other railways use various methods such as a mechanised conveyor belt, the bucket of a JCB, or simply shovelling the black stuff from the coal stage straight into the bunker. Just a few standard-

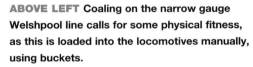

ABOVE LEFT Coaling on the narrow gauge Welshpool line calls for some physical fitness, as this is loaded into the locomotives manually, using buckets.

ABOVE The high-sided bunkers of the Welsh Highland Railway's Garratt locomotives are filled very simply by using a tractor with a front-loading bucket.

LEFT Only a few standard-gauge lines possess the large overhead coal drops as used in the steam age, as here at Grosmont on the North Yorkshire Moors Railway.

gauge lines have the large coal drops that were once commonplace in the steam age.

On hot, dry days it is a good idea to run a hose over the bunker or tender to damp down the coal and prevent coal dust flying about. The other aspect to check is that the shovel is not in the coal space when you start to fill it. I have suffered from trying to fire a trip with a buried shovel blocking half the coal door, accompanied by disapproving looks from the driver.

With the locomotive prepared, coaled and watered, it is time to attach it to the train, and to then build up the fire and water while awaiting the guard's whistle. On the Llanfair line the trick is to have the water gauge at least half full – three quarters being ideal – and the pressure gauge close to the red line, just as departure time arrives. What you don't want is so big a fire that the safety valves lift in stations as that is a big no no. While building the fire, you want to keep it off the front of the firebox, to prevent the engine from making visible smoke in the station, as we will explain during our next section on firing technique.

As previously mentioned, this is the procedure on one particular railway and other lines will have different methods, particularly standard-gauge lines where in some cases, for example, volunteers will be rostered purely as fire lighters. The fireman's duties might also encompass other tasks. Traditionally on British Railways for instance, the fireman was responsible for collecting the lubricating oil at the start of the shift and placing it on a plate in the cab where it could be warmed by the fire ready for the driver's use. Also, if the locomotive was fitted with a hydrostatic lubricator it was the fireman's responsibility to check its level and refill as necessary. We will look at lubrication later. As your footplate career proceeds you will soon pick up what is expected of you on your particular line.

The fireman's duties – on the road

I started this chapter describing a common misconception of the fireman's role on the footplate. In fact, firing a steam locomotive is a juggling act, trying to provide the right amount of heat and water to produce the steam pressure needed for the driver's requirements, whilst taking into account the weight of the train, the route and particularly its gradients, the track conditions, the weather, whether the carriage steam heating is being used, how long ago the locomotive had a wash out, even how the driver handles his locomotive. Since the end

LEFT Ready to go. The fire is a healthy orange colour, and there is plenty of water showing in the gauges, so departure should be soon.

ABOVE RIGHT On the footplate of a standard-gauge tender engine, the driver has his eye on the road and the fireman has plenty of space to swing the shovel and feed the large firebox. *(Alan Crotty)*

RIGHT On a 15in-gauge locomotive there is no problem with having room to swing, but the driver has to do the firing too! *(Alan Crotty)*

COUPLING UP

Coupling and uncoupling a locomotive from its train is very much part of the fireman's duties. They will use hand signals to enable the driver to ease the locomotive on to the end of the train, and then step between the locomotive and rolling stock to perform the actual coupling process.

On most standard-gauge lines there are two main coupling formats, the traditional screw coupling, and the more modern buckeye. On narrow-gauge lines there is more variety, although most tend to be either versions of the screw coupling or the 'chopper', all of which are described on the following pages.

Hand signals are an essential part of communications between driver and fireman when the latter is off the engine. The fireman uses such signals to see the locomotive on to the train. Hand signals should be given to an agreed standard format.

1 A hand moved towards and across the body, at about shoulder level, means: 'approach the hand signal'.
2 A hand moved away from and across the body, at about shoulder level, means: 'move away from the hand signal'.
3 Holding the arm horizontally across the body, moving the hand up and down means: 'continue the previous manoeuvre but more slowly, ready to stop'.
4 Holding both hands up in the air means 'stop'. It is important that you use both arms for this manoeuvre and only one for

RIGHT Hand signals.

1 One arm held vertically signifies 'all right'.
2 One arm moved in a circular motion away from the body signifies 'move away'.
3 One arm moved across and towards the body at shoulder height signifies 'come towards'.
4 One arm held out horizontally with the hand moving up and down signifies 'slow down'.
5 Both hands held directly above the head signify 'stop'. This is the only signal using both arms, so the driver on seeing the second arm start to move has an early warning that they must stop.
6 An arm moved vertically up and down above the shoulder signifies 'create vacuum'.

FAR LEFT A screw coupling, seen hanging from the bufferbeam of a standard-gauge locomotive.

LEFT The buckeye coupling is used to join standard-gauge passenger stock together and can require some skill and strength to couple and uncouple if being done by hand, rather than automatically. This coupler is in the stored position with the hook at its top to enable the vehicle to be coupled to the locomotive which is not fitted with a buckeye.

the others, keeping the unused arm by your side, as the initial movement of the second arm gives the driver an early warning that you are about to tell him to stop.

5 A vertically downwards motion with one hand tells the driver to create vacuum once the fireman has connected the vacuum brake pipes.

The screw coupling

The screw coupling is a virtually standard fit on standard-gauge locomotives, and consists of a pair of buckles, permanently attached to a hook on the locomotive bufferbeam and adjusted by a screw mechanism fitted between the buckles. Thanks to a weight on the adjustment arm the coupling hangs vertically downwards when not in use.

With this type of coupling the driver will bring his locomotive gently against the stock, known as 'buffering up' and causing the two pairs of spring-loaded buffers to gently compress slightly on contact with each other.

Having confirmed with the driver that all movement has ceased, the fireman first disconnects the vacuum brake pipes from their dollies and then lifts the end of the coupling over the hook on the other vehicle. That vehicle's own coupling is not used and is left hanging. If the driver has stopped correctly the coupling on the hook should hang slack, slightly less than horizontal and the fireman then uses the adjustment arm to tighten

the coupling to the horizontal, taking up the slack. Finally, he connects the vacuum pipes, grabbing an end in either hand and joining them through a twisting motion.

When uncoupling, the procedure is carried out in reverse, requiring the driver to first move the locomotive very slightly towards its train, compressing the buffers before the handbrake is applied and the fireman can then go between the vehicles to uncouple them.

A more simple version, usually found on older goods stock, is the three-link coupling. This consists of three chain links, the end one simply placed over the hook on the next vehicle. With no screw-tightening mechanism the couplings remain slack, which is why they can only be used for good trains, leading to the expression 'loose-coupled freight'.

The buckeye coupling

The buckeye coupling is a very common device and has been a standard fit on standard-gauge passenger stock for many years, and is still used on the mainline today. With many redundant carriages finding their way to heritage lines it has become equally familiar among volunteer train crews. The buckeye is an automatic unit, and while considered the most modern coupling, it was invented in America as long ago as 1879.

The only time a locomotive crew may need to operate the buckeye will be if joining or splitting parts of a train, as locomotives are coupled to

RIGHT This training
aid, seen in the
museum at the Gwili
Railway in South
Wales, shows the
buckeye coupling
when coupled
together. In full-size
form this view is
normally hidden by the
corridor connections
of carriages.

BELOW In the UK, the
Grondana coupling is
unique to the narrow
gauge Welshpool
& Llanfair Light
Railway, but is similar
in principle to other
screw couplings. It
combines a centre
buffer with a separate
shackle, which is
placed over hooks
and tightened.

their trains by means of their screw couplings.
The buckeye includes a hook as in the screw
coupling, but from it hangs a large cast steel
head containing a hinged jaw or knuckle.
This head has two positions, down (hanging
vertically), and up (horizontal) with a securing
pin securing it in either position. Moving the
coupling up to the horizontal requires a particular
technique that the fireman will be taught, as it
can weigh around 90 kilos (198lb)!

To join two vehicles both couplings are lifted
into their up positions and at least one of the
knuckles opened. This is achieved by lifting
a locking pin on the coupling, releasing the

knuckle. As the two vehicles come together
the knuckles of the two couplings close around
each other and will stay joined. To release them,
a chain is pulled on one of the buckeyes and the
locking pin lifted which releases a block inside
the coupler causing the knuckle to swing open.

Coupling typical standard-gauge passenger
vehicles together requires several other tasks.
As well as connecting the vacuum brake pipes
there are often electrical connections to join,
and most obviously, the corridor connections
allowing passengers to move between carriages.
For this reason, some standard-gauge lines,
particularly larger ones, include a passenger
shunter role among their operating staff.

Coupling on the narrow gauge

The major difference between standard-gauge
and most traditional narrow-gauge lines is that
very little narrow-gauge stock uses a twin buffer
arrangement. The standard arrangement is a
single, centre buffer which is combined with a
coupling. There are exceptions – preservation
pioneer the Talyllyn Railway is the best known,
with its twin-buffer arrangement, but the
techniques used are the same as for the
centre coupler.

The coupling itself can be of varying types
such as a screw as on the standard gauge (the
main difference being that the buckle and screw
is a separate unit not permanently attached to
the locomotive), a link and pin arrangement and
the chopper, or Norwegian, coupling.

Screw couplings

The Grondana coupling originated in Sierra
Leone and is today unique to the Welshpool &
Llanfair Light Railway in Mid-Wales. It is similar
in format to combined single centre buffers
and couplers as used on many narrow-gauge
railways but the coupling process is similar
to that on a standard-gauge locomotive.
The buffers of the locomotive and stock
are brought together, and the fireman steps
between the vehicles, pulling off the vacuum
brakes on both. The coupler unit is placed
over the hooks on both the buffer shanks and
the shackle is then tightened until the coupling
is level and just tight enough to start pulling
the hooks together. Finally, the vacuum pipes
are reconnected.

LEFT This is the simple link-and-pin coupling with two pins placed at each end of a chain link to hold vehicles together. On this example, fitted to the tender of a Ravenglass & Eskdale Railway 15in-gauge locomotive, a metal plate is used in preference to a chain.

ABOVE This link-and-pin coupling, fitted to a narrow-gauge quarry Hunslet locomotive, has three alternative heights for the chain, to cater for varying heights of stock and standards of track, particularly in the quarries.

Link and pin coupling

The link and pin is a simple unit. The centre buffer has a horizontal slot in it, into which is placed a chain link. It is then secured at both ends by a vertical pin inserted through a hole in the top of each buffer. Popular on early narrow-gauge lines and still used on some smaller lines today, its main disadvantage is a fairly loose connection with a degree of slack built in.

Chopper coupling

The chopper coupling found very wide application on narrow-gauge lines. It consists of a large hook (looking a lot like a meat cleaver, hence the name chopper) pivoting on a horizontal bar built into the top of the centre buffer. When swung to the horizontal the hook holds on to the bar of its opposite number. A pin can be used to secure the coupling in the horizontal.

The chopper is not regarded as the strongest coupling around and stock fitted with it often boasts auxiliary chains as an additional safeguard. Most narrow-gauge lines do not have turning facilities for rolling stock, so with stock always facing the same direction some choppers have the hook fitted on only one end, the other having only the locating pin in the buffer.

FAR LEFT The chopper coupling, with the hook (the 'chopper') clearly visible in its off position, pivoted back on its bar. To couple up this grabs the bar of its opposite number, keeping the vehicles together.

LEFT Here, a chopper coupling is being joined, with the two hooks being persuaded to grab the bars. *(Eddie Bellass)*

of regular steam on the mainlines, that juggling act has, if anything, increased.

In the old, pre-preservation days, locomotives were generally fired on coal with known qualities, Welsh steam coal or Yorkshire coal, whereas today the black lumps can come from anywhere around the world, particularly from the former Soviet republics. On the Welshpool line, each succeeding batch of coal delivered can be totally different to the previous, in how quickly it burns, how long before it produces heat, how long it lasts, how much smoke it produces, and how easily it is prone to produce ash or particularly clinker. We will learn more about the evil that is clinker later.

When you first step up on to the footplate the art of firing will appear, well, as a black art, which at times you will believe you can never master. You may well, during your time as a trainee, share a footplate with many different firemen, all of whom will have their own variation of the basic method, which they will of course insist is the only right way. You will have bad days, when you will leave the shed in the evening vowing never to go back, but you will go back and then you will have a good day. Remember this is your hobby and you are supposed to enjoy it!

In short, good firing technique comes through experience, and you have plenty of time to gain this experience and form your own preferred technique. You are not in a race to learn. What the following description can do is give you some of the basics on which you can build that technique.

In simple terms, you put coal into the fire on the grate, which produces hot gases, and these

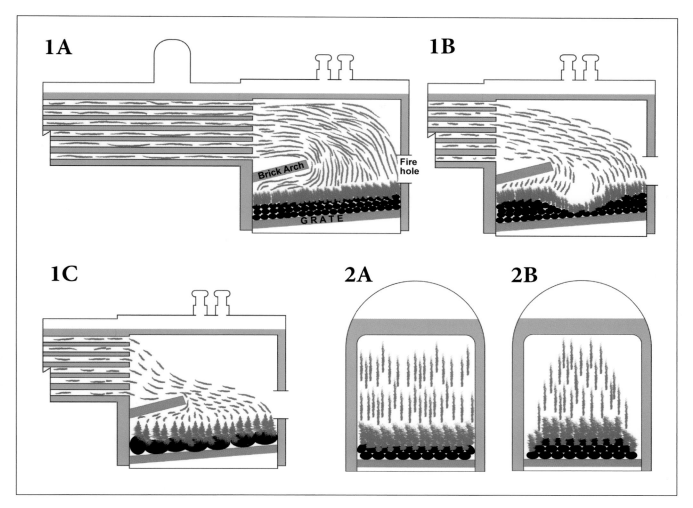

are drawn through the boiler tubes to boil the water and make the steam. The art is to first ensure that the fire stays alight (I'm not joking) and secondly, to control the fire in such a way that it burns at its most efficient, producing the most hot gases for the least fuel used. Also ever more a concern in these modern times, is producing the cleanest exhaust – in other words, making the least visible smoke possible.

Coal and air

First, we need to understand what we are burning. Of the constituents that make up a lump of coal, by far the majority is carbon. The rest are gases: oxygen, hydrogen and nitrogen, and sulphur and ash. When the carbon and hydrogen in the coal are combined with oxygen in the air heat is given off. Coal begins burning at about 800°F (427°C) but will not burn efficiently until it reaches very much higher temperatures. If the oxygen level in the air is correct, combining

ABOVE

In 1A an even firebed covers the entire grate with no thin or dead spots letting in excess primary air from below. This allows every inch of the firebox combustion space to be used and all combustion to be completed in the firebox.

In 1B an uneven firebed, with a 'hump', often caused by the fireman not projecting coal far enough along the box, leads to over-thick areas with no air space under the door and at the front of the box with thin patches in the middle allowing in excess air and gaps in the flame. Combustion will not be completed in the box and the loco will produce thick black smoke.

In 1C the effect of over-large lumps of coal can be seen producing an uneven firebed, there are gaps in the flames, and inefficient use of the combustion space.

The view looking forward in 2A shows an even firebed allowing combustion to take place across the full width of the firebox. A 'humped' firebed as in 2B leads to less efficient combustion. The centre is too thick while there are thin areas at the edges letting in too much primary air. This often occurs on narrow gauge locomotives with wide, short fireboxes in which the rear corners of the box can often be out of sight of the fireman.

this with the carbon produces a colourless gas called carbon dioxide, while the combination of the hydrogen and the oxygen produces water vapour, or steam.

If there is too little air, however, carbon monoxide is produced, a poisonous gas which provides only around 30 per cent of the available heat. At correct temperatures, around 2,500°F (1,370°C), the coal burns at its most efficient and splits into two main parts. The first are gaseous compounds of hydrogen and carbon, known as hydrocarbons, the second is solid matter, coke, which remains behind and produces the waste ash. If, however, the temperature is correct, but too little oxygen is available in the form of air, some hydro-carbons escape up the chimney, causing dense smoke in the process.

To summarise, having lit up as described earlier, keeping your fire going at its most efficient basically requires the right combination of coal and air. So, how is this achieved in the firebox?

In firebox terms, there are two types of air and two phrases you will have etched on your mind. **Primary** air is that which is drawn through the fire from below the grate and is controlled by the dampers. **Secondary** air is supplied from above the fire through the firehole door in the cab.

Too much air will lead to a loss of heat, and this is easily judged by looking at the chimney. If the exhaust is clear then there is too much air, unless you are standing in a station for a long period, or just arriving after a long journey. A clear exhaust is a sure sign that you need to give the air something to combust with. In other words, you need to put more coal on the fire.

Right, let's turn theory into practice. On the road, your simple aim at all times is to have the boiler pressure as close as possible to the red line on the pressure gauge, the point where the safety valves lift without actually letting them blow and wasting your hard-earned steam. This is done by controlling the fire and therefore the heat, and the amount of water in the boiler by using the injectors. More of which in a moment.

Firing technique

Firing technique is affected by the type of locomotive you are firing, for example, whether it has a long, narrow firebox, or a short-wide

one, or whether it has a brick arch (see page 42). While brick arches are very common in standard-gauge locomotives, most narrow-gauge engines do without them. Your firing technique will improve as you become experienced with the particular idiosyncrasies of the locomotives on your line.

Some firemen swear by the 'horseshoe' technique where the fire is arranged so that it is thicker at the back and sides of the firebox. At this point we should mention that when referring to a firebox, the front is always towards the boiler (the front of the locomotive), the back is closest to the firehole door.

Generally, an evenly spaced fire tends to work best in providing the heat you require with, perhaps, a slight thickening towards the back. Some engines respond well to thinner fires than others, but if you keep your fire thin you always run the risk of holes forming in it where the coal has burned right through to the firebars. This will allow an excess amount of primary air through the firebox, lowering its temperature, so such holes need to be filled quickly.

Holes can also be pulled in the fire by the locomotive slipping. This creates a strong vacuum or 'pull' on the fire, and the holes appear. On locomotives fitted with wide, deep fireboxes, it is easy to miss seeing such holes forming in the back corners and under the door where they are not so obvious. An extra round of coal put across the back of the box can often pay dividends here. A likely sign of a hole is a nasty rumbling sound that you will hear as the locomotive passes over a bridge or a culvert when an excess of air is pulled up through the grate.

A popular phrase among firemen is 'little and often', achieved by adding coal on a regular basis, but not too much at a time. A bad fireman will fill the box with a great mass of coal and then leave it to sort itself out. As coal absorbs heat, firing this way tends to drop the temperature of the fire, leading to it burning unevenly and the combustion process being constricted. This procedure also produces smoke – thick black smoke at the chimney, which is a sure sign of over-firing.

It is a good idea to adopt a routine to ensure that you fill the fire bed evenly. Some firemen say you should start what is a methodical

technique by filling the back of the box. However, if you do this, you will then have to peer through the flames of the freshly burning coal to see where the coal needs to go in the front of the box. A good sign of an area ready to be filled is that the flames are lighter and brighter compared with those surrounding them. 'When the fire is white the fire is light', the old firemen used to say.

So, your first rounds of coal may be applied across the front of the box, going left front corner, right front corner, then a couple of shovelfuls in the middle under the tubeplate, one biased to the left and the other to the right. The second session will be the same but across the middle, then across the back, ensuring you get right into the corners and then placing rounds under the door, one by flicking the shovel to the left, the others by tilting the shovel to the right. By this time the front will be nearly burnt through and ready for more.

There is a technique to wielding the shovel too, especially on standard-gauge engines with long fireboxes where you will have to learn how to put enough swing in your shovel action to actually get the coal to the front of the grate. A common problem is to find yourself aiming coal at the very front of the grate but landing it only two-thirds of the way in. This produces a hump in the fire which, as well as encouraging uneven burning, also cuts the space to pitch through to reach the front of the grate – especially if there is a brick arch above the hump!

One of my trainers, an ex-British Railways fireman, showed me a technique where, when he swung the shovel he banged it on the bottom of the firehole, thus sending the coal in an arc through the box and to the front. On our narrow-gauge engines space is at a premium and early in my training I actually changed my firing technique from left-handed to right-handed, simply to avoid getting in the way of the driver. Our locomotives are all driven from the right of the cab.

On standard-gauge engines there may be much more room to get a good swing in, but they are also of greatly varied cab layouts, and may be driven from the left or right. With the loco fleet on many of today's preserved lines having come from a range of sources, the fireman may have to be ambidextrous. On smaller narrow-gauge engines there is such a lack of space that the fireman only adds coal at stations, often through a hole in the cab backplate. Going even smaller, on the miniature lines the driver will also be the fireman, although he won't need to do any swinging, simply spooning in coal as needed.

When firing the back corners of the firebox you must really flick the coal into the corner as a half-hearted attempt will land it a little way up the box and not right where it's wanted, encouraging the formation of a hole. If you hold the back of the shovel with your palm over it, the shovel will more naturally turn to the right and with your palm under it, to the left. For firing under the door, don't just trickle the coal in, as again, you will miss the back of the grate. Turn the shovel sharply over, first to the left then to the right, banging the rear upper part of the shoved on the bottom of the firehole as you do to pitch the coal straight downwards.

Knowledge of the route you are taking is essential, as there are good and bad times to fire. You should never fire when starting away, as the fire will not be at a very high temperature and you want to raise that temperature. Opening the firehole door and lumping coal on at this point will drop the temperature, whereas keeping the door shut, thus ensuring the most primary air is drawn to the fire from below helped by open dampers, and if necessary, some extra pull from the blower, will bring the fire's temperature up ready for a round of coal.

The best time to fire is when the engine is running at a constant speed and the driver has notched up a gear. In other words, the reverser has been moved closer to its central point. You should avoid firing when the engine is working hard, as there will be a strong pull on the fire from the chimney and every time you open the firehole door you will pull in unwanted cooling secondary air.

From the above you will see that 'knowing the road' – the route on which you are working – is important to firing in the most efficient manner. You need to know where the gradients, the ups and downs are, as this will indicate when the driver will be using the regulator or otherwise. But it is also vital for the safety of yourself and your driver to know where you will be passing over bridges, or through tunnels. Running over a bridge or a culvert can greatly increase the amount of air flowing through the grate from underneath. Running through a tunnel, meanwhile, can cause a pressure pulse in the chimney. Both situations are the recipe for a 'blowback' where, if one opens the firehole door, flames leap

out of the opening, potentially filling the cab with fire. Blowbacks can also be caused by the smokebox door being opened, destroying the vacuum. A good technique is never to completely close the blower, having it at least cracked slightly open helps to avoid blowbacks.

Clearly, opening the firehole door as little as possible is an advantage. On our small narrow-gauge locomotives it is possible to fire one-handed, allowing you to use the other hand to open the door as you swing the shovel at it, closing the door straight after thus minimising the amount of air drawn in. This is not really practical on the larger standard-gauge engines however.

The chimney is an excellent barometer of the state of your fire. When on the road, a clear exhaust suggests you need to get some coal on. If you do it correctly, then in around 15 to 20 seconds (the type of coal affecting this time) a light grey smoke should appear from the chimney. As already stated, if it all goes thick and dark you are over doing it. You can also tell by looking carefully at the exhaust if the

BELOW The combination of light smoke emerging from the chimney and steam from the safety valves of 'Merchant Navy' class 4-6-2 No. 35027 *Port Line* at West Hoathly on the Bluebell Railway, suggests the fire is burning well. This is a good thing as the fireman would have needed to have kept his firehole door firmly shut while running through the long tunnel here.

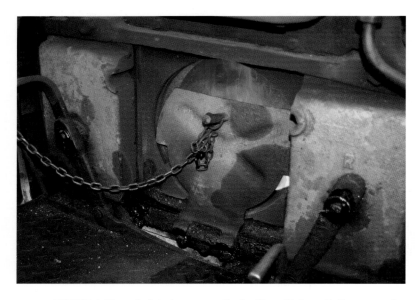

ABOVE A hinged plate known as the baffle, which partially covers the firehole but allows cooling secondary air to enter over its top, is one aid to controlling an over-enthusiastic fire.

BELOW This interesting view shows the different states of the fire in two locomotives at the Statfold Barn Railway. The white smoke from the chimney of the leading quarry Hunslet, 0-4-0ST *Statfold*, built as recently as 2005, suggests the latest round of coal has been burning for a little while. The much darker exhaust of the following Orenstein & Koppel 0-6-0WT+T *Sragi 14* of 1923 suggests the fireman has just put a round of coal on the fire.

fire is being over-fired on one side of the grate compared to the other, and adjust accordingly. The smoke can actually appear to be coming out of only one side of the chimney.

Of course, when standing in a station, making smoke is frowned upon, and a way to avoid this is to fire only occasionally and with the emphasis on one side of the grate. The heat on the hotter side then helps to prevent the cooler side from making smoke while the thin side also ensures there is not an excess of heat when it is not needed. Similarly, you should decrease your firing towards the end of the run to ensure you don't arrive at the shed with a huge roaring fire.

There are ways of controlling the air entering the firebox. As mentioned earlier, primary air enters below by means of the dampers, the hinged plates fitted to the front and rear of the ash pan. Secondary air enters by opening the firehole door. Most engines also have a baffle, which is a hinged metal plate that, when the firehole door is open, can be hinged upwards to cover most but not all of the opening. This also has the advantage of keeping temperatures down on the footplate, particularly on smaller locomotives with little space.

These are important tools as the fire can burn too efficiently thereby creating more steam than the driver needs. The trick, as previously stated, is to have the steam pressure as close as possible to the red line where the safety valves will lift, so that the driver has all the pressure available he can use. Having the safety valves constantly lifting however, is a situation approved of only by lineside photographers. So, as well as controlling the rate of heat and steam production through the use of dampers, the blower and the firehole door, a prime way of controlling excessive steam pressure is to use the injectors. These devices have a more important role, however, in replacing the boiler water that has been turned into steam.

A good fireman will have one eye on the pressure gauge, the other on the water gauge. It is of course essential that the water level in the boiler does not drop too low, with the

ABOVE British Railways Standard Class 4MT 4-6-0 *The Green Knight,* built in 1954, has just arrived at Whitby station on a working from Pickering on the North Yorkshire Moors Railway. The lack of visible smoke at the chimney is the sign of a conscientious fireman.

LEFT British Railways Class 8P 4-6-2 No. 71000 *Duke of Gloucester,* built in 1954, will be delighting the photographers following a mainline railtour, with its visually dramatic plume of steam. However, the fireman will prefer to keep the pressure gauge just below the red line which indicates when the safety valves will lift. (Eddie Bellass)

CLINKER

RIGHT The fireman's enemy – clinker, a mass of fused, poorly burnt coal and ash. In this form it can be broken up and lifted off the firebed, but when it gets larger and sticks to the firebars the fireman has problems.

BELOW Careful use of the fire-irons to clean the fire is key to avoiding clinker, no matter what the size of locomotive. This is the 15in-gauge Romney, Hythe & Dymchurch Railway in Kent.

Clinker is the enemy of the fireman. It is formed when poorly burning lumps of coal fuse together to form a substance that lies across the firebars and strangles the air flow, thereby increasing the problem. Some types of coal are more prone to forming clinker than others and a visual sign of it potentially happening is a blue flame, as opposed to orange or white, visible in the firebox. If steam pressure is struggling, even with dampers wide open, looking for clinker will be a good idea.

If there is clinker in the firebox it needs to be found and removed as the problem will simply magnify if ignored. This is where the fire irons are employed. If you know the coal your railway is using is prone to clinkering, it is worth having a look in the box while standing at a station, as the irons are easier to handle when the locomotive is not on the move.

As described earlier the fire irons are big, heavy iron bars. The dart is straight and looks like a spear while the pricker has an end turned through 90 degrees. They can be used in various ways to locate clinker, lift it from the firebars and either break it up, if possible, or lift it out of the box, either by working it on to the shovel or using a set of clinker tongs.

However, the irons should always be used sparingly, as they are themselves cold compared with the fire and in stirring it up you run the risk of lowering the temperature and further encouraging the formation of clinker.

Clinker disposal is not an easy or a particularly enjoyable operation. Make sure you wear gloves as metal tools placed in a very hot fire will quickly become hot themselves. The iron is carefully worked through the fire, the aim being to get under the burning coals to the firebars where clinker might lay. It is a job you need to learn particularly, for example, in locomotives with small fireboxes. With thinner fires you don't want to knock your fire through the grate. A good idea is to do half the box at a time, first placing some fresh, reasonably sized lumps of coal on one half, then checking the other half. By the time you've finished the new coal will likely be burning and can be pushed on to the holes in the firebed that you have no doubt created. You then do the other half, topping up with fresh coal when you've finished.

danger of exposing the firebox crown and melting the fusible plugs. Accurately reading the gauge will take some time to master. Up or down gradients cause the level to bob up and down, as will the application of brakes or sudden acceleration.

Use of the injectors

Locomotives are usually fitted with two injectors, one on the fireman's side and the other on the driver's side. Each has two separate controls, a water valve and a steam valve, both of which can be controlled by wheels or levers. With the live-steam injector the procedure is to turn the water valve on, producing a stream of water out of the overflow pipe alongside the base of the cab, followed by the steam valve. The dropping water disappears accompanied by a raspy sound as the steam forces the water into the boiler under pressure. Sometimes the water continues to dribble out of the overflow pipe, but this can be 'trimmed' using the lever/wheel of the water valve. When the injector is in use the overflow pipe needs to be kept an eye on as sometimes the injector can 'drop off', which is evidenced by the fast flow resuming from the overflow pipe.

A locomotive may instead be fitted with exhaust-steam injectors, which re-use the steam after it has done its work in the cylinders, rather than simply sending it straight up the chimney. They will also work with live steam and have an advantage in that the water injected into the boiler will be hot and, as a result, will be more quickly turned to steam thus cutting the locomotive's fuel consumption.

To operate an exhaust-steam injector the steam spindle is opened to about 90 degrees, which admits live steam from the boiler to operate valves in the injector. This allows water into the injector, producing a visible flow from the overflow which once spotted is a sign to open the steam spindle fully, starting the injector, which may still need trimming.

If the locomotive is working with a supply of exhaust steam, the act of opening the steam spindle also operates an exhaust steam valve in the injector body allowing steam taken from the smokebox to power the injector. This steam will have droplets of lubricant in it picked up when in the cylinder, so a separator removes this

RIGHT The simplest form of colour-light signal: a two-aspect with red below and green above.

SIGNALS

Signalling forms a vast, complex subject and has resulted in many a book. As a footplate crew member you will need to have a working knowledge of the signalling on your line, even if you are not a driver. The fireman is a back-up to the driver and on occasions will call out the position of signals if they are first visible from their side of the cab.

Modern signals are of course based on colour lights, in many ways similar to traffic lights. Colour-light signals can come in two-aspect (two bulb), three-aspect or four-aspect varieties, the last being very rare on preserved steam lines.

The working of two-aspect signals is obvious: red means stop, as the line ahead is occupied; green, not surprisingly, means line is clear ahead. A three-aspect places an amber light between red and green. If the signal is showing amber, it signifies that the section ahead is clear but the one after that is occupied. It can be passed, but the driver will be pre-warned that the next signal may well be showing red, requiring the train to stop. Four-aspect simply adds a second amber light; both on together tells the driver two sections ahead are clear.

There are colour lights on some of today's steam lines, but the vast majority use the form of signalling that has held sway for much of railway history (and which can still be seen on some mainline routes even today) – the semaphore.

The semaphore signal is quite simply a rectangular plate or arm placed at the top of a post which pivots at one end, moving from danger (horizontal), to clear. This can be up (on upper-quadrant signals) or down (lower-quadrant). Earlier versions, and those used by the Great Western Railway, were lower quadrant, until one winter the weight of snow on a signal placed at danger forced its arm down to clear, resulting in an accident. After this the upper-quadrant eventually became the

RIGHT Even in this black-and-white photograph from the days of steam showing former War Department 2-8-0 No. 90212 reversing into Parkside Colliery, Newton-on-Willows, the distinct differences between the home (top) and distant (below) signals on the poles at the left can be seen. *(Eddie Bellass)*

standard, although there are still many lower-quadrant signals in use today.

The signal arm includes two lenses at its pivot end. They are coloured clear or green and red, and depending on the position of the arm, one or the other will be illuminated by a lamp mounted on the post allowing the signal to be read at night.

There are two basic types of semaphore signal, the home and distant. The arms of home signals are coloured red with a vertical white stripe, while those of distant signals are yellow with a black stripe, along with a forked outer end to the arm. Home signals must be obeyed: if the arm is at danger the train must stop. Distant signals, however, serve simply as a warning. A distant signal at danger can be passed, the driver knowing that the next home signal is also likely to be showing danger and must be stopped at.

Both home and distant signals can be placed on the same posts (the distant referring to the next home signal along the line). Semaphore signals can also come in multi-posted varieties. For example, where a siding or loop diverges from the mainline, a two-armed signal will be provided with the arm for the siding/loop placed lower than that for the mainline.

Sidings can also have their own much smaller versions of the semaphore – these are

placed low down at the side of the track, and are called ground signals. These have the home arm painted on a metal disc that moves from danger to clear.

There are many other types of semaphore signals such as the 'calling-on signal' for example. This is a much smaller arm mounted low on a signal post, with a white horizontal stripe on a red background to specify when a locomotive can move on to its train standing in the station platform. Such complexities are outside the scope of this book, but those interested in learning more will find suggested further reading at the back of the book.

ABOVE The signals are against 1944-built Stanier 'Black Five' 4-6-0 No. 44806 on the North Yorkshire Moors Railway, with a variety of home arms on display. The lower-mounted arms protect sidings or loops, while the small arms with horizontal white stripes are 'calling-on' signals for movements within station limits.

LEFT A typical home semaphore signal. The larger upper arm instructs the train to move past it on the mainline, whereas the smaller, lower arm, is for moving around within station limits, for example, running into the loop to coal up.

BELOW A ground signal, as placed on sidings and loops.

lubricant before it can contaminate the water being injected. If this was not done it could cause the boiler to prime, as detailed in the driving chapter.

Each time water is put into the boiler by means of the injectors some steam pressure is used up. How much will depend on how long you have the injector on and how big the injector's capacity is. Therefore, steam pressure rising too close to the red line on the gauge can be controlled by the use of the injector, but only to a point.

Having too much water in the boiler can be as dangerous as having too little, as it can lead to priming. This occurs when water is carried out of the boiler through the regulator and the steam passages to the cylinders. It will be visible as dirty, black droplets around the chimney cap, and these drops can be projected skywards, rapidly making a mess of both locomotive and rolling stock. Far more

seriously, however, the excess water can reach the cylinders and cause great damage when compressed by the pistons. In the worst cases, the end of the cylinder could be blown clean off. We will learn more about coping with priming in the next chapter.

More duties on the road

The fireman's duties stretch a long way beyond providing steam for the driver's use. They are half of a team that work together, and the fireman has several more tasks to perform. For a start, from their point on the footplate the driver can only see forward down one side of the locomotive, back down one side of the train. Therefore it is up to the fireman to regularly check the other side (especially in station areas where there might be people standing close to the locomotive), and to confirm to the driver that all is well.

The fireman also checks the line ahead as

on many of today's single-track preserved lines and particularly on curves, the fireman can often see further along the line, spotting obstructions or the position of signals before the driver can. They are therefore able to give an early warning of any problems.

Another example of the fireman's role involves the staff and ticket or electric token system used to ensure safety on single-track lines, as detailed on the following pages. These rely on the driver having the correct staff, ticket or token for the line section being entered, and on receiving it (usually from a signalman) he should routinely show it to the fireman to get a confirmation from a second pair of eyes.

Finally, at the end of the run, there are a number of duties that both the fireman and driver need to carry out in order to 'put the loco to bed'. The process, known as disposal, is yet another example of team work and the very last activity of hopefully a successful day on the footplate, so we will describe this process at the end of the book, after the section on driving.

How it used to be – by Frank Podmore

More from 1950s British Railways Southern Region fireman Frank Podmore, this time on preparing a locomotive for a run.

The locomotive would have been lit up at the shed before the fireman, who was going to take it on the train, began his turn. So, on entering the cab the fireman's duties were as follows:

- Check the fire and if necessary, spread it across the bed.
- Check the water level in the boiler.
- Collect the oil for the cylinders and lubricator, and paraffin from the stores.
- Put the cylinder oil on the tray above the firehole door to keep it warm.
- Check the tools. There should be four spanners, four lamps, four white discs (used on Southern Region as a daytime replacement for lamps), a brush, bucket, detonators (for placing on the line to warn other trains should the locomotive break down while on the route), the oil feeder for the driver, the coal pick and the fire irons (two shovels, two prickers and two darts, on larger locomotives).
- Check the smokebox for cleanliness and tightness, check the ash pan is clean, the water level in the tender or tanks, and clean the cab windows.
- Fill, clean, trim and light (if necessary) the lamps and place on the front and rear of the locomotive. On the SR, white discs substituted for the lamps in daylight.
- Fill the lubricator.
- Trim the coal, sweep up, and dust and hose down.
- Clean the gauge glasses, the gauge lamp and boiler backhead.
- Build up the fire and fill with water to ensure you are able to be off shed at the appointed time.

The fireman would generally take about an hour to properly prepare a large locomotive for the journey.

ABOVE A close-up of the staff-and-ticket system used on the Welshpool & Llanfair Light Railway. A single staff and ticket for the section of line between Cyfronydd and Castle Caereinion stations are shown detached from their holder. The line is divided into four coloured sections, while the staff for each section is of hexagonal section, the ticket is square.

RIGHT Welshpool & Llanfair staffs and tickets in their holder. With this, the driver will be able to take his train from Llanfair Caereinion to Castle Caereinion, the mid-point of the line. To continue from Castle through the remaining two sections to the other terminus at Welshpool, he will need the staffs and tickets coloured black and green, which are missing from this holder because they are with a train that is currently on that section of line. The key-like device on the holder is an Annett's key, as used by the blockman at the crossing point to unlock and change the points.

RIGHT The controller on the Welshpool & Llanfair Light Railway is about to hand the staffs and tickets, in their holder, to the footplate crew. Only two of the four colour-coded sections are present. This is because another train is out on the line and the two will cross at the halfway point of the line, their staffs and tickets being swapped over.

Signalling is an essential element of keeping trains safely apart, but there is also a fail-safe method of train control which can be used even when there are no signals, such as is often the case on narrow-gauge railways. On single lines, where trains run in both directions on the same track (as do most of today's heritage railways), it is essential, and it is called the token system or block working.

In this system the railway line is divided into sections, each of which has its own specific token or staff. This is a physical object, usually metal, which has to be in the possession of the driver before he can enter the section. As there is only one token for each section, it follows that there is no chance of two trains meeting on the single line.

However, this system has limitations as it requires trains to be run in opposite directions one after the other, whereas it might be required to run two (or more) trains in one direction before a return train brings the staff back to its starting point. Making this possible is an enhanced version of the staff, known as the staff-and-ticket.

The driver is issued with a ticket enabling him

to take his train through the section or block, but can only depart if he has been shown the staff when he receives the ticket. The final train through the section before one is due in the other direction takes the staff with it. No train will be able to come the other way with a ticket, because it will be impossible to show the driver the staff before he proceeds.

Improvements in technology and particularly the arrival of electricity, eventually enabled the staff-and-ticket to evolve into a much more flexible system, known as the electric train staff. In this setup, a machine containing several tokens is placed at each end of a line section. This is linked electrically to an identical machine at the other end of the section. As soon as a token is withdrawn from either of the machines they lock, preventing the removal of any more tokens until the withdrawn one is replaced at either end. This way, any number of trains can proceed in one direction, but only one at a time as only one token can be issued at a time.

Today, most heritage lines are divided into block sections and you will often observe the handover of authority to proceed through a section, whether it is a ticket, a staff or an electric token, often in a pouch, between footplate

ABOVE A pair of colour-coded, electric token machines which protect two different sections on the Talyllyn Railway. If a token is drawn out of either machine no more can be withdrawn until the first token is either replaced in the machine, or in the equivalent machine at the other end of the section. *(Walter Crowe)*

crew and signalman or controller. Training on your particular line will include becoming totally competent with whichever system of token is used, and until you are, you will not pass out as a footplate crew member. It is essential to the efficient and safe running of your line.

LEFT A close-up of a single electric token instrument with the various tokens visible in their slots. *(Richard Hayden)*

BELOW The footplate crew of LMS 'Jubilee' class 4-6-0 *Leander* are receiving the token from the signalman, their authority to proceed along the next section of the East Lancashire Railway. *(Eddie Bellass)*

Chapter Five

Driving a steam locomotive

Finally – the holy grail of the footplate career. Driving a steam locomotive is the ultimate ambition of many enthusiasts, from the moment they first step on to a footplate. To take charge of such a beast of a machine, no matter what its size, and to control it, produces a level of satisfaction hard to match.

OPPOSITE In this view of a standard-gauge cab can be seen not only the regulator, but a screw-type reverser on which the driver is resting his hand. *(Cliff Thomas)*

ABOVE Driving a
steam locomotive
is the ultimate level
of working on the
footplate, but brings
with it responsibilities.
(Tom White)

controlled merely by means of a hand on a vacuum brake. On a major standard-gauge line such as the Severn Valley, that tonnage rate can increase to well over 300.

While the guard is considered in charge of the train, the driver is in charge of the locomotive and is responsible for its safe and efficient working, and this includes overseeing the fireman. He therefore also needs the mental skills of being able to effectively manage his colleague, ensuring the locomotive is worked to its best ability, having sufficient steam pressure available when needed while not blowing off excessively especially at stations, and all the while maintaining a pleasant relationship with his colleague. It's all about teamwork and some drivers can finish a day's turn as mentally exhausted as the fireman may be physically.

The status of driver is not what all footplate crew desire and many of today's enthusiasts reach the level of fireman and are quite happy to stay there, not wanting the extra responsibility that comes with being a driver. That is fine as it is easy to forget that today's steam locomotive crews are primarily there not to put food on the table, but as part of a very enjoyable hobby.

As with firemen, different railways have varying methods of promotion to driving standard. Some still follow the regimented procedure that was the case in the days of British Railways and before. The aspiring driver works his way up through the grades of fireman and passed fireman, with a set number of turns required at each level before consideration for the next level. Others have a less rigid procedure, with potential driver candidates identified by senior loco crew and encouraged accordingly. The one common feature that every aspiring driver will require if they are to progress, is the support and appreciation of their peers in the loco department. At the end of the day, as we have already stated, this is teamwork.

We saw in the chapter on firing that the most effective way to demonstrate the skills that a driver requires is to work through a typical day on that side of the footplate, explaining each aspect of the role as it is carried out.

Just like the fireman, the driver's first task at the start of a 'turn' is to sign on. He may well be doing this somewhat later than his

However, the fact that this chapter falls so late in a book titled *The Steam Locomotive Driver's Manual* demonstrates just how skilled a task drivers undertake, and how much commitment in both time and enthusiasm is necessary to reach this stage of one's footplate career. It is not for everyone as driving a locomotive on regular train services comes with heavy responsibilities, to a level one simply does not encounter on say a one-day footplate course.

To give one example, even on my narrow-gauge Welshpool & Llanfair Light Railway, descending the 1-in-29 Golfa Bank on a damp day with a loaded train, the driver can have behind his locomotive some 50 tonnes or more, containing hundreds of passengers, and

colleague, who will require much more time to prepare the locomotive and light it up, but the driver will follow a similar procedure in the office of checking for any new notices and standing orders. In particular he will look at the notices for any potential technical issues reported on the locomotive that will be in his charge for the day.

On reaching the shed the driver will first climb on to the footplate, checking that the handbrake is on, the regulator is closed, the reverser is in mid gear, and the water gauge is showing a sufficient level in the boiler, probably 'bobbing' the level to make sure. He will also check the steam pressure gauge, particularly in the morning following lighting-up, to ensure the loco will be ready when required for its train, along with other checks that should have been already made by the fireman. This includes the level of water in the tanks, the presence of the spark arrestor, and the proper sealing of the smokebox door. By checking these things again the driver both backs up his colleague's work and also satisfies himself as to the safe condition of the locomotive, particularly as he is about to work down in its motion.

Different railways today again have different procedures regarding the driver's visual inspection. On my line for example, the inspection is divided into two: the start of day and end of day. When signing on, the driver will have checked if an end-of-day inspection was carried out by the last crew on the locomotive. If not, he will need to incorporate that into his start-of-day inspection.

For this reason, it is prudent to look at an end-of-day inspection first. On the Welshpool line this is carried out over an inspection pit and includes looking first at the condition of the springs. A broken spring leaf can be an immediate cause for failing the engine and taking it out of traffic. It is not always the case if the problem is just one leaf in the middle of the 'pack' as it may be decided that the loco can run with it and have the spring replaced at the end of its turn. However, one of the large, major leaves will need immediate replacement.

LEFT **With the loco over the pit the driver can walk under it and, with the aid of a torch, get a good look at such areas as the internal motion.**

ABOVE **The condition of springs is easier to observe on some locomotives compared with others!**

Other areas clearly visible from under the loco and needing to be checked include the spring hangers, the brake linkage, horn keeps, drain cock linkage and damper linkage, and the condition or even presence of the various locknuts and split pins securing components in all these areas. Generally, the driver is hunting for anything amiss, and clearly a locomotive kept as clean as possible makes spotting any defects a lot easier.

Even if he knows the locomotive had an end-of-day inspection last time out, the driver will still usually want to have a look underneath, over the pit, as part of his start-of-day inspection. But otherwise, the examination concentrates on areas accessible from above track level, and the driver will now check every element of the motion, usually combining this task with

LEFT **Leaf springs are life-limited items and railways maintain stocks of replacements, such as this range of various sizes on the North Yorkshire Moors Railway.**

BELOW **Just this small section of locomotive requires a wide number of checks, from the tightness of nuts and split pins to the integrity of the leaf spring, and whether such major parts as the wheel balance weight at left have not become loosened.**

LEFT A torch is an essential aid to the driver as he checks the less visible areas of the loco's bottom end, here looking at the top of an axlebox.

lubrication, as detailed below. He will be using his eyes to spot visual signs of anything that is not well, while also performing such basic tasks as grabbing hold of parts of the motion to check they are secure, and taking up the wear on such areas as big ends if needed.

Obvious visual indicators of problems include loose rivets, pins or bolts, and split pins that are either not tight with the ends bent open, or are missing altogether. There are also less obvious but important tell-tale signs of other potential problems. While we constantly remind readers that a locomotive should be kept clean, traces of unusual brightness against dull metal are an alarm bell. On areas with bearings, such as axleboxes, big ends or rods, crank pins and such like, evidence of whitemetal can suggest the bearing has been running hot. This is usually through inadequate lubrication. A thin strip of bright metal on a part that is riveted or bolted together, such as the balance weights on wheels, suggests that the part is loose.

The evidence does not have to be bright. Traces of rust around a rivet or bolt are evidence that it is broken. Evidence of emulsified oil close to a piston gland is a sure sign that the gland in question is blowing.

As the driver conducts his inspection he will have close at hand a hammer and a spanner, usually of the adjustable variety. The hammer is to tap various joints, bolts and the like, extending from the motion right up to the mating surfaces of vacuum or air pipes, listening

LEFT The driver's check includes observing the condition of the various split pins located throughout the locomotive's running gear.

LEFT A hammer is used to tap various joints and bolts in the motion, ensuring that they 'ring true'.

RIGHT On this locomotive, fitted with vacuum brakes, the ends of the hoses are checked for integrity by tapping them with the hammer.

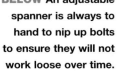

BELOW An adjustable spanner is always to hand to nip up bolts to ensure they will not work loose over time.

for the sound that comes back. Just as with the famed wheel tappers of the steam age, a bolt or similar with a crack in it will produce a different sound to one that is healthy as it will not 'ring true'.

The adjustable spanner, meanwhile, serves an obvious purpose. Bolts employed in a constantly moving environment such as in the motion will work themselves loose over time, so before each turn the driver takes care to ensure everything is secure, 'nipping up' any bolts that need tightening.

Working methodically to a pre-set pattern, the driver should be able to check the entire locomotive for anything amiss, while performing the essential lubricating as he goes.

Lubrication

Lubrication is of course a major element of the operation of a steam locomotive, and is a role primarily carried out by the driver. However, on some railways still following traditional methods, the fireman may be responsible for collecting the lubricating oil from the stores. Once brought to the locomotive the oil cans will normally be placed on a flat plate directly above the firehole door. This is the 'warming plate', which as its title suggests, warms the thick oil to lessen its viscosity and make it flow more easily into the various oiling points on the locomotive.

As described in the how-it-works chapter, there are two distinct types of oil used on a locomotive. One lubricates the various bearing surfaces, such as in the motion, and the other thicker oil, is pumped or injected into the cylinders to lubricate their inside surfaces, as well as being used to lubricate the steam brake. This is traditionally known as cylinder oil although it is colloquially described as steam oil. Back in the days of steam on the mainline there were two types, one thicker than the other and designed for the greater heat demands of superheated locomotives. Today's lubricant

LEFT The oil cans are placed on a metal plate located directly above the firehole door, allowing them to warm and reduce the viscosity of the lubricant.

LEFT The mechanical lubricator is carefully filled with cylinder or steam oil…

BELOW …and then its handle is rotated to 'prime' it, pumping the oil through the system. This should be visible through the sight glass at the top of the lubricator.

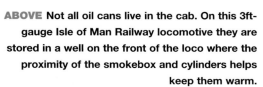

ABOVE Not all oil cans live in the cab. On this 3ft-gauge Isle of Man Railway locomotive they are stored in a well on the front of the loco where the proximity of the smokebox and cylinders helps keep them warm.

technology has removed the need for two different types.

The driver will normally fill the lubricators requiring cylinder/steam oil first, giving the thicker liquid the most time to warm through and lessen its viscosity for easier flow. Typically, a mechanical lubricator is filled to its sight glass and then manually operated or primed by turning its handle to ensure the oil is pumping through correctly. The moving oil should be visible through the sight glass.

If the locomotive is fitted with a hydrostatic lubricator, as are for example many Great Western Railway engines as illustrated in Chapter 2, then traditionally replenishing it falls within the fireman's duties. With the lubricator's steam feed and admissions valves closed, water is drained from it by first opening a cock on the bottom of the body, which should release any pressure in the system, and then removing a hexagon-shaped filler nut on the top of the body using a specific spanner. Steam oil is poured in until its level reaches the base of the filler nut thread, the nut is replaced and the steam valve reopened. There is another cock which allows steam to flow

RIGHT AND FAR RIGHT This is a typical oil box. In the open position the trimmings are visible in the bath of oil.

RIGHT A worsted trimming is withdrawn from its oil cup. The oil runs down the trimming and into the feeder hole.

RIGHT Checking the trimmings is essential to ensure they are correctly siphoning the oil.

through the lubricator body, warming the oil before it is used.

The driver then moves to the lubrication of the various moving parts, usually combining 'oiling round' with his visual checks of the motion. There are three methods of movement on the locomotive that require lubrication: the part either rotates, such as in the bearings of an axlebox or the ends of a coupling rod; it slides, as in crossheads, valves and the like, or it rocks, such as the little end of a connecting rod, which rocks on the crosshead, or the union link from the crosshead to the combination lever. The type of lubrication fitting varies accordingly.

The sliding parts generally have a feed from a cup or pot located above the part in question, and in the bottom of which is contained a trimming made of worsted yarn. The yarn draws out the oil from the pot by a syphon action, and then feeds it to the moving component, a drop at a time.

There are three types of these trimmings The simplest is the **Plug**, which simply fits directly into the feed hole to restrict the flow of oil. The **Plug Tail** draws the oil out of the pot or cup, providing a more consistent flow to the oiling point. Finally, there is the **Tail**, which is used where a greater flow of oil is required.

The rocking parts of the motion are usually fed from a well which has a pad made from worsted yarn in it. The pad regulates the flow of oil.

Rotating parts tend to need more oil and will have their own individual and larger cups mounted directly on the part itself, for example, above the big ends of connecting and coupling rods. The holes for these are sealed on the top with a cork, the advantage of this being that should the cork fall out it will not potentially cause damage to the motion in the way a metal cap could. Trimming these corks to size with a penknife is another on the list of skills a driver needs to acquire! Some large locomotives, however, have a more complex system, with a spring-loaded ball sealing the hole.

Inside the cup is a restrictor plug which is either threaded or tapered, with flutes in the sides. Below the oil hole is at least one felt pad, and as the part rotates the oil is thrown around the cup, a certain amount being pushed through the flutes and on to the felt pad, maintaining constant lubrication, but only when it is needed, on the move.

Axleboxes will also often require water syphoning out of them before any oil pots are refilled, and so it is essential to check for water in any oil reservoirs. This water can be picked up on the road in wet weather, but can also be the result of a careless fireman overfilling the water tanks on a tank locomotive.

Generally, a two-cylinder Walschaerts locomotive is the easiest to oil round as its motion is all on the outside. On three-cylinder variants, and Stephenson Link-equipped engines for example, much of the motion is inside, which usually entails crawling amongst the motion while the locomotive is over an inspection pit. It is not so bad on narrow-gauge engines, where one can usually reach between the frames to access the oiling points, but clearly with any task involving areas inside the frames it is crucial to ensure there is no likelihood of the locomotive moving, or even the reverser being operated, changing the geometry of the motion.

Lubrication is a task that should be carried out in a methodical way to ensure none of the various oiling points are missed and, as mentioned earlier, the driver soon learns to combine this task with the visual examination, thus ensuring no part is left unchecked or unoiled. The number of oiling points and their location depends entirely on the design of the locomotive. A driver on the Mid-Hants Railway told the author that a British Railways Standard class locomotive, for example, can be oiled round in less than half the time it takes to do the same job on a Southern or Great

LEFT It is essential that oiling round is carried out methodically to ensure no points are missed.

Western Railway locomotive of similar size. Part of the reason for this was the widespread use of grease nipples on the later Standard locomotives, which are far more efficient and easier to deal with. Learning where the various oiling points are located on particular locomotives and how not to miss any of them forms a major part of the driver's training.

BELOW Corks are used to plug oil fillers as they are easily replaced.

ABOVE Larger oiling points, such as in the top of axleboxes, are fed by a pump-action lubricator.

RIGHT Great Western 'Hall' class *Olton Hall* is seen being oiled up at Crewe Loco Works. It is wearing the distinctive red livery in which it played a starring role in the *Harry Potter* films.
(Eddie Bellass)

If the previous crew were on their game the locomotive would have been left in the best position for its visual examination and subsequent oiling. This position can vary between types of motion and on locomotives with three cylinders and Walschaerts valve gear it is impossible to set the motion in order to be able to oil round all the points in one go. Traditionally on standard-gauge locomotives with the two most popular forms of motion – two-cylinder Walschaerts and Stephenson's Link – the 'right' position is with the big end of the leading connecting rod in the top back quarter of the wheel i.e. 'ten past', on the clock. This is not universal, however, as the Welshpool & Llanfair's Walschaerts-fitted narrow-gauge locomotives are left at 'twenty to' with the leading connecting rod's big end in the left bottom quarter of the wheel.

Whichever railway you work on you will be taught a 'preferred' position in which to leave the locomotive for oiling. The priority is to have the various oiling points of the motion in a position that makes them easiest to reach. They should not be blocked by other parts of motion in the way, while the oil cups in such components as the little ends should be tilted to a position where they will be able to accommodate the most amount of oil.

The popular method of examination/oiling is to start at the rearmost end of the left-hand coupling rod, working around the entire outside motion to finish at the equivalent rearmost end of the right-hand coupling rod. The same task is then performed on the inside motion, if the locomotive is so fitted.

Cleanliness is again essential. When filling the oil feeder cans and using them, they should be wiped to ensure no grit, ash or such like gets into the oil reservoir. Similarly, when one removes a cork, a wipe around its base first will get rid of any dirt that might be sitting on its edge. It is equally essential not to overfill the cup and this is done only to the base of the thread that secures the retaining cork, otherwise once on the move the pressure of the oil will force the cork out, with the oil following it. If a cup is overfilled, the simple way to remove the excess oil is to stick one's finger in the hole. This will push out the unwanted oil, which can then be wiped away with a rag. In any case,

having replaced the cork firmly and squarely in the hole, one should wipe the surroundings with a rag to keep dirt at bay.

If the locomotive is fitted with the spring-loaded ball type of retainer, a screwdriver or similar is needed to press down on the ball, exposing the hole for filling with oil. When the pressure is released the ball will spring back to its closed position. Again, ensure any excess oil is wiped away with a cloth.

There will be other checks the driver will make before the locomotive leaves the shed including making sure the sanders are full and operate correctly. When filling the sander it is essential not to spill the sand as it could easily find its way to areas where its abrasive nature will not be welcome, such as the bearing surfaces of motion parts. Any spillages around the sander should be cleaned up immediately.

Once suitable steam pressure is raised

ABOVE The sanders must be filled with high-quality sand from the stores, particularly if a damp day is forecast. When needed, the sand is dropped through a pipe just ahead of the wheel to aid grip on a slippery rail. The operation of the sanders should be checked before leaving the shed.

the driver will ensure that the injectors work correctly, a procedure fully described in the chapter on firing. He will also test the operation of the brakes, whether steam, vacuum or air (depending which system the line in question uses), along with the handbrake.

Driving the locomotive

With all the checks and the preparations done, it is time to indulge in that ultimate experience as a member of a footplate crew – moving the locomotive under your control. Obviously, by the time you attain the rank of a driver with only your fireman on the footplate for company, you will have driven locomotives many times and are likely have done so even before you officially started driver training. Whatever promotion hierarchy your particular heritage line uses, you will likely find that firemen, as they gain experience, are given regular chances to try the regulator for themselves.

Driving a steam locomotive requires the operation of three major controls: the regulator, the reverser, and the brake. These are the core controls in the cab and to offer an automotive analogy, the regulator is the accelerator, the reverser the gearbox, and the brakes, well, the brakes!

The regulator and the reverser

The regulator is usually a long lever which is either mounted in a quadrant frame vertically atop the back of the firebox and moves in an arc away from the driver's position, or is mounted horizontally on top of the firebox and moves, again in an arc, towards the driver. The two ends of its frame are generally marked 'shut' and 'open'. It connects by a shaft to the regulator valve which is often mounted in the locomotive's dome or sometimes in the smokebox. The vertically mounted regulator uses a shaft running through the boiler and is kept steam tight by packing known as the regulator gland. The pull-out type of regulator tends to have its linkage running outside the boiler, close to the top of it and connected directly to the regulator valve through steam-tight packing.

The regulator valve itself is also mounted horizontally or vertically. Horizontal ones allow the dome to be lower in height and as a result, the boiler itself can be larger in diameter while still fitting into the railway's loading gauge.

RIGHT A tank locomotive regulator handle. It has two ends and is designed to make it easiest to use while running both forwards and backwards.

By moving the regulator handle on the footplate, the valve is opened, allowing steam to pass through it and along pipes to the cylinders. In some locomotives it may, as explained in Chapter 2, pass through the superheater on the way. The body of the regulator has a flat face with ports cast into it, as does the slide that moves across the face, operated by the lever. With the regulator closed all the ports are out of line so no steam can pass to the cylinders. Moving the lever brings the ports into line one by one, and when the first are lined up the regulator is regarded as being in 'first' or 'pilot' valve. Moving the regulator handle further, to make the locomotive produce more power, lines up all the ports, and the regulator is described as being in 'main valve'.

The reverser can be of two types. By far the most common is a lever mounted vertically on a toothed quadrant. Squeezing the handle on the top of the lever pulls the catch clear of the quadrant and allows the reverser to be moved through the teeth, or notches, as they are known. The number of notches is the same either side of the vertical or closed position, which is referred to as mid gear. Unlike a car, a steam locomotive is expected to work as efficiently in reverse as it does moving forwards.

The bottom of the lever is directly connected by a rod to the locomotive's motion, and changing the position of the lever changes the geometry of the motion. This is both in terms of the direction in which it works the locomotive, and more pertinently, the amount the steam valve travels along the valve chest before stopping steam being admitted to the cylinder: the 'cut off'. With the locomotive in 'full gear' with the reverser either right at the front or back of the quadrant, the greatest amount of steam is let into the cylinders, typically for 75 per cent of the stroke.

As the locomotive gathers speed, however, the reverser is moved closer to its mid-point, reducing the valve travel and admitting less steam and allowing full expansion of steam already in the cylinder to take place, so the locomotive can operate more efficiently. Very loosely, full forward or backward gear can be considered equivalent to selecting first gear in a car. One moves up through the notches towards the centre of the reverser, just as

LEFT A pole-type reversing lever. Squeezing the catch at the top enables it to be moved across the notches in its quadrant. On this Welshpool & Llanfair locomotive the lever is unusually mounted on the fireman's side of the cab.

one changes up through the gears in a car as it increases in speed. Also, just like one depresses the clutch in a car when changing gear, it can be necessary to momentarily close the regulator when moving the lever, due to the pressure of steam on the valve chest in the cylinders.

The less-common type of reverser replaces the lever with a screw handle arrangement, particularly on larger locomotives where the forces produced by a large moving set of motion can make a lever reverser harder to operate. The screw reverser is slower to operate than the lever type as the equivalent of moving through notches requires many turns of the handle. According to steam-age locoman Frank Podmore, the reverser on a British Railways Standard type locomotive took 28 turns from full forward to full reverse, and was known colloquially as the 'bacon slicer'. However, such reversers offer finer degrees of control than do the lever type.

Moving the locomotive out of the shed at the start of the turn requires immediate use of both the regulator and the reverser. To start with we will know that the reverser is in mid-gear, the regulator is closed, the drain cocks are open and the handbrake is on. As previously

described, both driver and fireman would have checked these more than once. The first step is to apply the locomotive's steam brake, then to release the handbrake. Blowing the whistle is an acknowledged safety move so this is done before any movement of a locomotive, whether with a train or running light engine. A check is made that no-one is standing in a position of danger around the engine, especially on the side you cannot see when at the regulator. This is a time to make use of your fireman as an extra pair of eyes.

The reverser is applied fully in the direction one wishes to go, and then the regulator is gently opened a little. Some resistance will be felt as the first or pilot valve opens, and this will be accompanied by steam issuing from the drain cocks as any built-up condensate is forced out of the cylinders. The regulator will be stiff initially due to the pressure of steam against it, but as it is opened more fully it becomes easier to operate and more sensitive as a result. The driver has to adjust his technique accordingly.

It is worth noting that an oft-practised start-of-day technique, when the locomotive has

been standing idle for a long period, is to put the reverser in the opposite direction to that wished to travel initially, and open the regulator very slightly, just enough to admit some steam to the cylinders, but not enough to move the locomotive. This is to ensure all condensate is cleared from both ends of the cylinder.

As the regulator is opened a little more the locomotive will start to move very slowly. You will see droplets of water both in the steam from the drain cocks and at the chimney top, and only when this clears is it safe to close the drain cocks. While photographers like the visual effect of open drain cocks, you don't want to use them any longer than necessary as when they are open the mechanical lubricator is cut off.

The technique is carried out in just the same way when starting with a loaded train, although obviously the locomotive is required to do a lot more. First of course, the driver does not make his own decision when to start away as that comes courtesy of the guard, who is in charge of the train and is responsible for it leaving the station on time. When they are ready the guard will blow a whistle to alert the locomotive crew, but this is not a signal to depart, merely to draw attention to them.

At this point, the train brakes will be partially released and the reverser placed fully in the direction that the train intends to go, ready for a prompt departure when given the signal. That signal is the 'right away', the waving of a green flag by the guard. It could be to the driver but equally to the fireman if the driver's position is on the opposite side of the cab to the platform when he relies on his colleague to look for the signal.

Having got the right away from the guard, the driver should still not move the train until he has assured himself that the signals are clear for the road ahead, and he is in possession of any staff, ticket or token required for the section of line he is entering.

As the locomotive begins to pull away, it is important for the footplate crew to look back, both to ensure that the guard has stepped on to the train safely and to see that no late passengers are attempting to board the moving train.

Pulling away with a loaded train requires the same basic procedure as with a light engine,

LEFT The green flag is the guard's signal to the driver that the train may leave. However, the driver will still need to check the road and the signals ahead before proceeding.

BELOW Starting away with a loaded train requires a gentle hand on the regulator to ensure a smooth getaway with no slipping, especially on a damp day. Here, Stanier 'Black Five' 4-6-0 No. 44806 eases out of Grosmont on the North Yorkshire Moors Railway with its drain cocks open for the first few yards.

RIGHT Progress is steady initially as the loco moves its train over the points and on to the mainline, as here with an LMS 'Crab' 2-6-0 departing from Ramsbottom on the East Lancs Railway. The starter signal is just visible in the 'off' position, something the driver would have checked before starting the loco. *(Eddie Bellass)*

BELOW When the weather is poor the smoke and steam from the departing loco will hang in the air, as on this wet day on the North Yorkshire Moors Railway. The footplate crew need to be extra vigilant in keeping their eyes on the road.

only there is of course a lot more weight involved. One has to exert very finely judged control with the regulator, especially on a damp rail or a gradient, as it is easy to make the locomotive 'slip'. This is when its wheels lose traction with the rail and spin without going anywhere. We will look at this phenomenon in detail shortly.

As the locomotive gathers speed, the reverser can be 'notched up', ie, moved closer to its mid-point. It is important to match the position of the reverser with the amount of power one is asking for through operation of the regulator. By admitting too much steam it will not be given sufficient space or time to expand fully in the cylinder. This is wasteful, particularly as it leads to a more pronounced 'blast' at the chimney, pulling the fire through the locomotive

LEFT As the locomotive gathers speed the driver will 'notch up', balancing regulator movements with those on the reverser. *(Cliff Thomas)*

at too high a rate and increasing coal and water consumption as a result.

Speed

One technique the aspiring driver will need to master at an early stage is maintaining a correct speed. The majority of steam locomotives are not fitted with speedometers, but the driver will come to judge the correct speed by experience.

In the past, aids to this learning process have included judging speed by the telegraph poles placed by the side of the line, as in the days of steam, these were always positioned a certain distance apart and it was possible to calculate one's speed from the time taken to pass them. The sound made from running over joints in the then standard-length rails could be used in a similar way.

LEFT Very few of today's steam locomotive footplate crews will experience speeds such as this. 'Battle of Britain' class Bulleid Pacific *Tangmere* heads a 'Pines Express' steam charter on the mainline. *(Eddie Bellass)*

Today, telegraph poles are far less common
and rail joints can vary enormously in length,
some lines even using continuous welded rail,
but with most heritage railways having a general
line speed of 15mph (although some are faster,
up to the realms of 25mph) one traditional aid
remains – the milepost at the side of the line.
These are placed every quarter of a mile, and
the distance travelled from the terminus marked
on them.

The designs of these posts varied according
to the railway. Some have the miles on the top
with the quarter, half, or three-quarter on the

side, while others show the miles as a number
with up to three vertical strokes for the quarters
under it. For example, 4 III would be 4¾ of
a mile from the start of the line. Travelling at
15mph one covers a mile in four minutes, so
if the trainee driver aims to cover the distance
between two mileposts in one minute, he
knows he is travelling at approximately 15mph.

One minute is, however, still a long time to
calculate and getting it short by just 15 seconds
results in travelling at some 20mph. The driver
with experience learns to judge his speed by
the sound that the locomotive makes as it

runs over the joints in the rails, and the general way that it rides. The Welshpool engines, for example, will start to exhibit a gentle sideways motion as speed rises beyond a certain point. Before long, judging speed becomes second nature, and slowing down to the 10mph or even 5mph required for a speed restriction (such as in station limits, running over facing points, or travelling over permanent way work) becomes easy to judge.

Most lines will have speed restrictions, both permanent ones marked by a signpost showing the lower speed limit and temporary ones (usually in areas where track maintenance is being carried out or potential line problems have been identified). These are marked by a signpost at the start of the restricted length showing either the letter C (Commence) or the reduced speed required, and T (terminate) at the end of the length. Usually, the speed limit across such temporary restrictions is 5mph or 10mph, and it is important to note that at the end of such a restriction the locomotive should not start to accelerate until the last vehicle of the train clears the T board.

Running over points is always something to be carried out with great care, especially when they are facing (i.e. the second line diverges away ahead of the loco). On some heritage lines, particularly narrow-gauge ones, points can be sprung-loaded to avoid the need for levers or a signalbox. This is notably in such areas as reverse loops where the point will be set against the train entering from the trailing direction, but the weight of the train will force the blades over to the correct position, the blades then springing back once the train has passed. A train should never stop on a sprung point, as the blade can swing back between the sets of wheels and unintentionally rolling back even slightly, can cause a derailment.

The brakes

While the new driver may enjoy bowling along at the controls of a steam locomotive, he will soon enough have to arrest its progress and slow it to a halt. Efficient brakes are of course essential for the safe operation of all locomotives, and as described in Chapter 2 there are various types, the operation of which the driver must be fully conversant with.

When running light engine, the driver will use a combination of the locomotive's brakes – usually a steam brake – and the handbrake. When attached to a passenger train he will be using those of the stock being hauled.

On a heritage line goods train the stock will only have individual handbrakes. Although these can be applied for descending a steep gradient, more usually, the only brakes available on the move will be those on the locomotive and on the brake van at the rear of the train,

LEFT Braking a non-fitted goods train such as this one requires co-operation between the driver at the front of the train and the guard travelling in the brake van at the rear.

RIGHT Seen here are
the vacuum brake,
to the fore, and the
handle of the steam
brake, on the cab
side. The former will
be used to brake the
train, the latter when
the locomotive is
running light engine.

locomotive, stopping a loaded train requires rather more skill and experience. This remains true today even though heritage railways do not run trains at anything like the speeds that were commonplace in the days of BR steam.

On the locomotive footplate one cannot simply stand on the brake as one would in a car, with its rubber tyres. These are steel wheels running on steel rails, and it is all too easy for them to lose grip with each other, the train sliding along with its wheels locked. This can occur particularly if the rails are slippery, either due to wet weather, or because it is covered in the mush of autumn leaves dropped and crushed on the rail head. This can even happen in hot weather when the rail head becomes oily due to a lack of rain washing it clean. In the least severe cases the train might slide past a signal, committing the notorious SPAD – Signal Passed At Danger. On most heritage railways this could result in the driver being disciplined or even suspended. In the worst cases of course, the train could collide with whatever is beyond the point it is trying to stop at.

To achieve smooth and consistent braking, either slowing the train to the speed desired, or coming to a halt at the point required (usually either in a station with your train correctly at the platform or at a signal showing danger), calls for knowledge of the route first and foremost. This includes where there are ups, downs and significant curves, and the likely rail conditions. The latter can be the result of both the weather and where the rail is located. Track through a damp cutting for example is likely to be more slippery than that out in the open. Knowing where the gradients and the curves are on the route is essential as these can be used to slow the train, reducing the amount of braking required.

Clearly, the regulator should be shut before braking commences, and the reverser should be returned to full gear. The brakes can be applied quite firmly at first, while the train is running at speed to slow its pace, but as speed reduces the braking pressure increases in influence. Therefore application will need to be reduced in a gradual manner to ensure the train does not come to a sudden halt with a jolt, making life uncomfortable for the passengers.

Operation of the braking systems fitted to

and in which the guard travels. When the driver requires braking, he will sound three short blasts on his whistle to alert the guard to apply the brakes in his van. The loose-coupled freight stock will tend to bunch up behind the locomotive as its brakes are applied, so just before the train comes to a halt, the driver will gently release his brake, the action of the guard's brake at the rear stretching the couplings out again and preventing too much of a jolt when the train restarts.

The author has ridden in the last wagon of a gravity slate train on the Ffestiniog Railway, with no locomotive and only brakesmen riding on the foremost of the 30 or more wagons, to slow the train's progress down the continuous gradient. When the brakesmen applied their brakes, compressing the gap between the loose-coupled wagons, by the time the resultant compression reached me, it was a jolt of several feet and was quite painful!

The vast majority of trains on today's heritage railways are, however, passenger workings, and the stopping will be controlled by either the vacuum or air-brake system as also described in Chapter 2.

While it should not take too long for the trainee driver to master the braking of an individual today's passenger trains is carried out in a similar fashion, whether they work by vacuum or by air. Using a lever in the cab and monitoring progress on a gauge, the air pressure or the amount of vacuum, is gradually reduced, which applies the brakes throughout the train. As stated, the braking force is gradually reduced so as to gently bring the train to a standstill. On the Welshpool line for example, the vacuum pressure with the brakes off is 21in, and initial brake applications reduce this to around 15in, slowing the train gently.

Having slowed the train sufficiently when approaching Llanfair Caereinion station, the line's headquarters, with judgement it is possible to gently let the brake off and the train will roll to a smooth stop in the platform. The step of the leading carriage is then right by the fouling mark, which is the point beyond where one cannot go without making it impossible to run the locomotive around the train. The trick is to try to stop a passenger train with the vacuum brake needle rising from 15in back to 21in, and like most aspects of footplate life, it is a technique that one learns through experience.

Once the train has stopped it is essential to return the brake lever to its normal position, restoring the vacuum or pressure in the system to replenish the reservoirs in the brakes.

Unless the train or locomotive is likely to move off again promptly, the handbrake will then be applied and the locomotive's steam, vacuum or air brake taken off. Before the crew steps down from the footplate, the reverser should be placed in mid-gear and the drain cocks opened to prevent any steam building up in the cylinders.

Duties on the road

In the chapter on firing we have already described two of the driver's other core duties while on the footplate because they involve the fireman as well. These are looking out for, understanding and obeying signals, and ensuring one has the correct authority for the section of track ahead in the form of a staff, ticket or token. The driver is primarily responsible for these aspects of the journey, although he will always use the fireman as a backup check.

Just like the fireman, the driver needs to 'know the road' in order to take his train along the route most efficiently. He will of course,

ABOVE No matter what the size of the locomotive, the driver will be keeping an eye on both the pressure and water gauges, whether he has a fireman or he has to do everything himself, as here on the 15in-gauge Evesham Vale Light Railway.

BELOW The footplate crew need to be particularly vigilant when going over level crossings, especially on heritage railways where such crossings may not necessarily be protected by barriers, as here on the Welsh Highland Railway in Porthmadog town centre.

RIGHT AND FAR RIGHT Other signs the driver may need to keep an eye open for on some lines are gradient posts, giving a guide to where power and braking need to be applied accordingly, as well as whistle and speed boards. These are on all lines instructing the sounding of a whistle and the speed required to traverse a certain section of track, such as a farm crossing or similar. The experienced crew get to know the road and such boards merely become a reminder.

need to know where the gradients are in order to use the regulator and reverser where required so as not to lose speed climbing a hill, or make a runaway descent the other side. Some railways have posts by the lineside showing where the gradients are but many, particularly narrow-gauge lines, rely on the crew to know the route by experience.

The crew also need to know where there are danger points such as bridges, tunnels, and, in particular, crossings whether of roads or farm access to fields. The latter are particularly dangerous as they are not protected in the same way as a major road crossing, and a combination of a good lookout and sounding of the whistle is required.

As well as looking ahead the driver will, on a regular basis, look behind to ensure all is well with his train, and he must also monitor everything that is happening on his footplate. Principally this is the amount of steam pressure, the level of the water in the gauge, and generally how the locomotive is steaming. As detailed earlier, this can be affected by a number of elements from the quality of the coal to the weather, and the prowess or otherwise of the fireman.

There may be times where the more experienced driver will need to advise or even on occasions, instruct his fireman in order to maintain progress of the train.

Each time the train stops for any significant period, usually at the other end of the line

LEFT Arrival at the opposite end of the line is not a time of rest for the footplate crew. Here, on the Welshpool & Llanfair Light Railway, the fireman refills the tanks while the driver oils around the motion again.

RIGHT Something many of today's drivers face that their steam-age counterparts did not do so often is regularly running large locomotives tender-first on trains. Very few of today's heritage railways have turning facilities located at both ends of the line. *(Eddie Bellass)*

before returning, the driver will take the opportunity to inspect his locomotive, and go round it oiling in the same manner as described at the start of this chapter. Often, he will do this while the fireman is refilling the water tanks. He will also look for signs for any bearings or axleboxes 'running hot', by feeling them with the back of his hand. They should be warm but not uncomfortably so and a part that is hot suggests a lubrication problem. Just as in

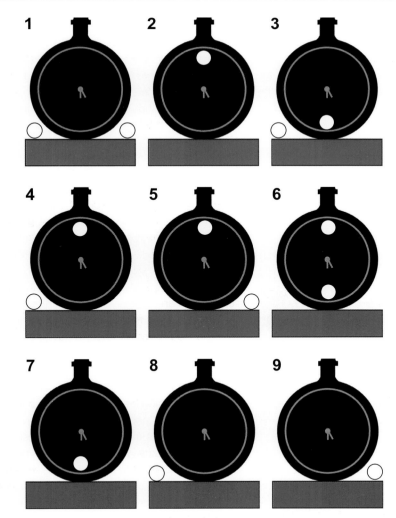

LEFT The placing of the lamps made it easy, particularly at night, to determine what type of train was approaching. Shown here is the generally accepted system of identifying locomotive headlamp codes used following the 1923 railway grouping. This was not completely standard, however. The Southern Railway for example, used its own five-lamp/disc system and some Scottish lines also had their own systems.

1 Express passenger train or breakdown train en route to an incident.
2 Stopping passenger train or breakdown train on way back to the depot.
3 Parcels, meat or perishables train of all carriage stock.
4 Empty stock or fitted freight with continuous brakes on at least a third of its length.
5 Express freight with less than one-third fitted stock.
6 Through freight or ballast train.
7 Light engine or engines coupled together.
8 Through mineral freight or empty wagons.
9 Short-distance freight or ballast train.

RIGHT Modern days have brought new challenges for steam locomotive footplate crew, as here at East Grinstead station on the Bluebell Railway.

NOTICE TO ENGINEMEN

NOISE & SMOKE MUST BE KEPT TO A MINIMUM AT EAST GRINSTEAD

AVOID ENGINE MOVEMENT WITH COCKS OPEN & USE OF INJECTORS NORTH OF PLATFORM

the shed at the start of the day, he will look for missing split pins, corks and the like.

If, on the next part of its journey, the loco will be running in the opposite direction than it arrived, one of the crew will need to move the head lamp. This sits on a bracket on the edge of the front footplate when going forwards, or on a similar bracket on the cab backsheet or the tender rear, when running in reverse. In daylight hours, some lines, notably the Southern Railway, used white discs instead of lamps. Several lamps were used in steam-age days, the order of their placing denoting what type of train they were on. This ranged from pickup goods to express passenger trains, and with even a distinct lamp code for the Royal Train.

At all times the conscientious driver will be looking for anything that could become a problem going forward. Like his fireman, he will be cleaning as he goes. Steam locomotives, by their very nature, can become dirty very quickly during a day's work and constant sweeping and wiping with rags helps to keep matters under control and to cut disposal time at the end of the day.

Locomotive problems

Slipping

While onlookers may find slipping dramatic and amusing, it is anything but desirable on the footplate. At the very least, the sudden extra draft created by an increase in motion speed can pull holes in the fire, but at its worst, the speed of the motion can increase out of control to a point where serious damage is done. This infamously happened to the express

passenger locomotive *Blue Peter* in 1994 when a violent slip combined with boiler priming (another no-no as we will describe shortly) to a point where the wheel speed reached 140mph, ripped the motion to pieces and blew the ends off the cylinders. The repairs took 18 months and extensive funds. A search of the online video service YouTube will reveal sobering footage of the incident.

If the locomotive slips it will be immediately obvious as the exhaust beat will become more rapid. The driver needs to shut the regulator immediately, hopefully arresting the slip before it gets too fast, and also before the train 'bunches' up, the couplings compressing behind the locomotive. At the least this can make for an uncomfortable ride for passengers as the couplings stretch again. The regulator is then opened more carefully, perhaps while using the sanders, to keep the train moving.

Sanding the rail, especially when it is damp, will help to prevent slipping, but this needs to be done sparingly as the abrasive sand greatly improves grip levels and as such can significantly increase the drag of a train. Sanders should also not be operated while a locomotive is slipping as the sudden restoration of grip can send a shock through the locomotive that can seriously damage it.

There are two types of sanders, the gravity-fed variety, common on smaller locomotives, and those fed by a jet of steam. Both types are controlled from the cab by means of a lever or a valve and the sand is deposited on the railhead just in front of the wheel needing the extra grip.

Priming

We first mentioned priming in the chapter on firing as it is a phenomenon in which the fireman is intimately involved. In simple terms it is the action of water going where only steam should – out of the boiler and into the cylinders. There are three potential causes: impurities in the water causing it either to foam or to lose its surface tension, and overfilling the boiler, either by forgetting that the injector is on, or using the injector too extensively to try to control an over-hot fire and prevent the safety valves lifting.

The first signs of priming are the exhaust changing to a more muffled beat, the smoke at the top of the chimney going whiter, and a fine

ABOVE The dirty deposits on the observation carriage window of this Welsh Highland Railway train show clearly that the locomotive is priming. Thankfully this was a mild example, but priming can be a very serious matter resulting in serious damage to the locomotive.

ABOVE At the end of the journey the fireman changes the points so the driver can run his locomotive around the train. Operations within station limits require particular care.

spray of soot-laden droplets emerging from the chimney. This dirties the locomotive, carriages and anyone standing close by. This is priming in its mildest form where water has passed from the boiler into the cylinders and is now being ejected through the blastpipe. It can become far more serious when water in the regulator can lock it, losing control of the locomotive and forcing larger amounts of water into the cylinders. The pistons are not able to compress the water to the same level that they do steam, with the result that the cylinder ends can be forced off, or the connecting rods bent.

If the locomotive starts to prime the regulator should be closed and the cylinder drain cocks opened in order to disperse the excess water. If the regulator is locked, the locomotive should be put into mid-gear after which it should be possible to close the regulator.

Locomotives vary in their tendency to prime, both through their mechanical layout and the quality of their fuel (coal and water) and also at what point they are in during their running cycle before washing out. This process described earlier, is carried out regularly to remove scale and other impurities from within the boiler. A competent crew will make every effort to avoid priming as it is by no means a desirable phenomenon.

SHUNTING

Moving a locomotive within station limits has to be carried out with particular caution, especially when buffering up to a train at the platform where there will be passengers and enthusiasts watching at close quarters. It is very likely passengers will be sitting in the carriages as the loco buffers up to them. A combination of the steam brake and handbrake is normally used to ease the loco into position on to the train, the driver closely following the hand signals given by whoever is giving the directions, this often being the fireman, as detailed in the chapter on firing.

It is essential the driver and fireman work as a team and are not distracted by those around them, even if they are good-natured onlookers asking questions just at the wrong moment. The fireman in particular should determine that all is safe with the locomotive and that the brakes are on, (usually indicated by a hand signal from the driver on the footplate), before he goes between the locomotive and the rolling stock to couple or uncouple it.

BELOW Shunting is something that must also be carried out with great care, using the hand signals described earlier in the book. Here, the fireman is making sure the driver can see him at all times.

Chapter Six

The end of the day – disposal

No matter how involving and how much fun each day on the footplate proves to be, eventually it has to come to an end, and for both driver and fireman there will be much work still to do after the final train has arrived at the terminus. Unlike a diesel locomotive, a steam engine cannot simply be driven into the shed and parked. There is a tried-and-tested set of procedures to be carried out known as disposal which are essential to ensure the locomotive is in prime condition for the crew when it is next used.

OPPOSITE Here, at Bressingham Steam Museum in Norfolk, the two locomotives are of different gauges, 2ft to the fore and 15in behind, but both are equally in need of an end-of-day blowdown.

149

The fireman in particular needs to be thinking about the end of day before that last train pulls into the terminus. He will manage his fire effectively as he will not want a raging inferno making plenty of steam when the locomotive is about to be put to bed for the night. So, in the latter stages of the final run he will be calming matters down, adding coal sparingly and just as closely, monitoring the water level in the boiler and the steam pressure. However, he won't want to go too far in the other direction for several reasons.

First, there may be shunting to be carried out after the last train, rearranging carriage sets for example. The particular railway may be one that blows down its locomotives at the end of the day, which as we will see shortly, needs a full gauge glass of water and enough pressure to replace it once the engine has been blown down. Even if the locomotive is not blown down there will be end-of-day procedures requiring a certain amount of steam pressure.

On many heritage railways, after being released from its last train of the day, the locomotive proceeds to take coal and water, simply because carrying out this task at this point reduces the amount of filling needed when the same procedure is carried out at the start of the next turn. It is also essential to ensure there is both enough water in the boiler and in the tanks to add to the boiler when the time comes to raise steam for the next turn.

Blowing down

We first encountered blowing down in the firing chapter as some lines, including my own Welshpool & Llanfair, carry out this procedure at the start of the day. Others, however, do it at the end of services, so we'll take a slightly more detailed look now.

The purpose of blowing down is simply to remove the impurities that are left behind when water is boiled. You can see examples of these, which are usually called scale, in any domestic kettle that has been well used. Water treatment added by the fireman when filling the tanks helps to control these impurities, but as more water is used they grow in extent, dropping to the bottom of the boiler barrel. This sediment can increase corrosion of the steel in the boiler, while the salts contained within the impurities can have an effect on the surface tension of the water in the boiler. If left behind, these impurities can result in the locomotive priming, as described in the previous chapter.

It should be added that blowing down is not a universal procedure, particularly on standard-gauge locomotives. Many of these are fitted with a continuous blowdown valve, which works all the time the locomotive's regulator is open, or the injectors are operating. The valve, powered by a pipe leading from the steam chest of the cylinders, takes a small amount of water from the boiler, just above the crown of the firebox, and deposits it into the ash pan, taking with it the waste impurities, and also helping to deaden the embers in the ash pan, cutting the possibility of stray embers escaping from the pan and starting fires. The valve is also connected to the injector, and the action of this working lifts valves within the blowdown valve allowing the water and waste to escape.

If the locomotive does not have a continuous blowdown valve, a regular blowdown regime is essential. This consists of the locomotive being parked and the driver opening a valve, usually located on the footplate, but in some cases it uses a handle under the boiler operated from the side of the locomotive. This forces steam and water out through a pipe at very high speed, and hopefully takes all the impurities with it. The pipe is located at the base of the boiler and many railways carry out their blowdown procedure over a specially designed drain between the rails.

To carry out a blowdown the driver needs a full glass of water with the level just visible in the top nut of the gauge glass. The fireman will be mindful of having enough steam pressure once the blowdown is complete to refill the boiler using the injectors, hence the requirement of careful boiler management on that last trip.

Before commencing the blowdown it is important to check the surroundings of the locomotive to ensure no-one is standing too close to it and especially not by the blowdown discharge pipe. Blowdown is a dramatic process that surrounds the locomotive in steam and also creates a great deal of noise and the use of ear defenders is recommended.

When the driver opens the blowdown valve water and steam rush out through the pipe and, in the author's experience, many drivers then immediately shut the valve again just to ensure it will shut off properly before commencing the main blowdown. The driver will typically blow down 'three quarters of a glass' watching the water level fall from full to a level of only quarter of the gauge glass. He will then shut off, at which point the fireman should be ready to replenish the boiler with water.

It is essential to keep a close eye on the blowdown procedure, as on some locomotives, the drop in water level happens very quickly and emptying the boiler of too much water could cause serious damage. It is also a good technique to check the blowdown valve has shut completely – one that hasn't is easily spotted by a telltale wisp of steam continuing to emerge from the discharge pipe.

Ashing out

The next procedure is ashing out. The ash pan will be raked out (or dropped if you are lucky enough to be dealing with a locomotive

boasting a hopper ash pan), in exactly the same way as carried out at the start of the turn. Apart from the toxic ash encouraging corrosion even if left in the pan just overnight, let alone any longer, an ash pan full of ash will be no aid to airflow when the next fireman is trying to light his fire.

A difference at the end of the day is that the smokebox also needs to be cleared, although it is worth noting that if the coal being used is of indifferent quality then it helps to ash out both the ash pan and smokebox at points during the day. Removal of ash from the smokebox is primarily to prevent corrosion.

In the final days of steam on British Railways, some locomotives were fitted with 'self-cleaning smokeboxes' which passed the ash through a number of processes then ejected it in small and harmless form through the chimney. Your locomotive is very unlikely to be so fitted, and there's no two ways about it, ashing out is a dirty job and if there's time it is worth changing back into your older overalls before starting.

BELOW Ashing out the smokebox is always done at the depot at the end of the day, but may also need to be done at other times, as seen here. *(Eddie Bellass)*

The smokebox door is opened, exactly as described in Chapter 4 and first, the distribution of ash on the floor of the smokebox is noted. An uneven pile of ash suggests there may be an air leak in the box, which will lead to poor steaming. The ash is then shovelled out, either directly into a pit if one is available, or into a wheelbarrow for later disposal. Particularly on narrow-gauge locos with their central buffer couplers, it is a good idea to cover the coupler with an old sheet to stop ash getting into its workings. Be careful when handling the shovel in the smokebox, as you don't want to dig into the fireclay that will usually be present helping to maintain the vacuum of the blastpipe. As you remove ash it is good to check the fireclay for any areas that may need repair.

Before finishing it is a good idea to brush the spark arrestor to remove any accumulated ash, but don't bash the mesh with the brush to loosen the ash as this will eventually break the mesh. Just as you did at the start of the turn, before closing the smokebox, brush around the base of the door and the smokebox ring to ensure a good tight seal.

After ashing out the locomotive will probably be taken over a pit so that the driver can carry out his end-of-day inspection. He will be looking for any potential items that need reporting in the fault book, for either dealing with by the next driver or, if more serious, by the workshop department, before the locomotive is used again.

While he is doing this it is essential for the fireman to keep the dampers closed so his colleague does not get a hot ember down the back of his neck. The fireman can busy himself during this period by sweeping around the cab footplate to ensure everything is clean as a locomotive should always be left as you would expect to find it when you first climb on to the footplate in the morning.

The locomotive then proceeds to its stabling point, either in a shed or a siding. At this point the injectors will be used to fill the boiler with water until the level just disappears above the top nut of the gauge. Doing this ensures that the next crew will have enough water in the boiler to light up the loco. As the water cools it compresses and the level will drop to the extent that there will be room to light up, but not so far that water has to be added to the boiler first. This is another reason why the fireman needs a certain amount of steam pressure left at the end of the day. It is desirable that the process of filling the boiler does not cause its pressure to drop too rapidly, as this means that the boiler will be cooled equally rapidly, placing unwanted thermal stresses on the metal.

For the same reason, very few railways throw out the entire contents of the firebox at the end of the day. Leaving at least part of the fire in the firebox, to die naturally, enables the boiler to cool slowly, negating those thermal stresses. Most firemen will rake the remains of the fire to cause the smaller embers to drop through to the ash pan, while leaving enough to keep things warm for as long as possible. This comes through experience, and it is equally important not to leave too big a fire in the box as the last thing you want on a locomotive that has been left for the night is for the pressure to start rising.

With the boiler filled a cap is placed on the chimney, which again, helps keep the heat in,

BELOW And so to bed. It's going to be a cold night, but the loco will be able to cool slowly in its shed following a good day's work.

the water gauge drained, and its cocks closed. Should an open gauge start leaking while the locomotive is stabled, or even worse, a gauge glass breaks, the next crew could be greeted by an empty boiler. It is also a good idea to drain any air reservoirs as they usually have their own small drain valves, to remove any condensation that might lead to corrosion.

A final check round is made to ensure all valves are shut, the regulator is closed, the handbrake firmly on and the reverser in mid-gear, so the locomotive can be left for the night. Then you the crew can head for the mess and a cup of tea, hopefully to reflect on an involving, challenging but above all thoroughly enjoyable day at the controls of a steam locomotive.

Summing up

Hopefully this book has unravelled some of the mysteries surrounding the operation of the steam locomotive, and has shown that today, more than it ever was during the steam age, climbing on to the footplate of a locomotive and taking control of it is a goal anyone who is fit and able, and with enough time and common sense, can achieve in their spare time as an enjoyable hobby.

A book, however detailed, can never reveal everything there is to know about life on the steam locomotive footplate. That will only come through experience, taking advantage of training sessions and mutual improvement classes, visiting other railways to see 'how it is done', and most essentially, listening to and learning from, the more experienced locomen you will work alongside. Some of these have now been driving locomotives on heritage railways for longer than their forebears would have done on the mainlines.

If you are reading these words while trying to decide whether you want to pursue your dream of driving a steam locomotive, then simply go for it, but just be prepared for this pastime to become all-involving.

BELOW Visiting the various heritage railway centres helps improve one's knowledge of footplate life, and beyond. This is the stores at the National Railway Museum in York, which is open to the public and for many, by far the most interesting part of the museum. It is full of educational material, such as the signals and lineside signs seen in this view.

RIGHT The small quarry Hunslet locos have traditionally been crewed by just one person, as they are today on the Launceston Steam Railway. Perhaps this is the first trip on the footplate for a lucky visitor to the popular Cornish railway. For the man on the left enjoying the ride, this could soon become an all-encompassing experience, whether in these less-than spacious surroundings…

BELOW …or crewing historic and varied locomotives such as on the pioneer Talyllyn Railway…

LEFT ...on a standard-gauge tank locomotive hauling a train on a line like the Dean Forest Railway...

BELOW ...or crewing enormous express passenger locomotives like this former LMS Stanier pairing. All will offer equal levels of enjoyment and satisfaction.
(Eddie Bellass)

Glossary

Some of the words associated with steam locomotive management

Air – primary and secondary – Primary air feeds the fire from below, being drawn in through the dampers and up through the grate. Secondary air is drawn in from above, through the firehole door, and cools the fire.

Air brake – A system which uses air pressure to apply the brakes on a train.

Ash pan – A metal tray under the fire grate which catches the fire's residue of ash and cinders, once the coal has burned through. It is usually emptied at the start and end of each turn. The ash pan has doors known as dampers (see below).

Backhead – The rear plate of the firebox projecting into the cab, on which are usually mounted the controls.

Baffle – A plate that can be raised to cover an open firehole door and help to control a fire, deflecting cold air coming through the door to keep it away from the tubeplate.

Balance weight – A large metal block attached to one side of a driving wheel which counteracts the reciprocal action of the crank on the other side.

Belpaire firebox – Popularised by G.J. Churchward of the Great Western Railway, this is a firebox with sides sloping outwards to a flat top, producing a larger, more efficient heating area.

Big end/Little end – The ends of a connecting rod in which the crank pins run.

Blastpipe – The pipe in the smokebox, which collects used steam from the cylinders and exhausts it vertically through the chimney. This action forms a draft, pulling hot gases from the fire through the boiler tubes.

Blinding – Ash particles covering the spark arrestor in the smokebox, restricting the airflow and causing bad steaming.

Blowdown valve – A valve that exhausts steam from the boiler, used to remove residue, such as scale, from it.

Blower – A steam jet mounted in the smokebox to create a forced draft to draw hot gases through the boiler tubes. It also prevents blowbacks of flame and smoke into the cab at times when the smokebox has no vacuum.

Bogie and pony trucks – A secondary set of wheels mounted ahead and/or behind coupled wheels of a locomotive to spread weight. Those with four wheels are known as bogies and those with two wheels are pony trucks.

Boiler barrel – The tube in which is held the water used to make steam. It is attached to the firebox at its rear and the smokebox at its front.

Boiler tube – Steel or copper tubes running through the boiler barrel from the firebox to the smokebox, through which hot gases are drawn to heat the water in the boiler and create steam.

Brick arch – An arch of firebricks fitted in the front of the firebox close to the boiler tubeplate, to aid combustion and to protect the tubeplate from fire.

Brightwork – A colloquial expression for parts of the locomotive in unpainted metal which require polishing to a bright finish.

Buckeye – A form of coupling used between standard-gauge carriages.

Bufferbeams – The front and rear plates of the locomotive frame, with buffers and couplers attached to them.

Bunker – The storage area usually at the back of the cab on a tank locomotive, in which coal or wood is stored.

Caprotti gear – Cam-driven valve gear, used on a few British Railways Standard locomotives. It is similar in principle to the cams in a car engine.

Chopper – A form of coupling widely used on the narrow gauge in which hooks on one vehicle engage in pins on the opposing vehicle.

Clack valves – Non-return valves placed between injector and boiler which automatically close when the injector is closed, to keep newly admitted water in the boiler.

Clinker – Residue produced when poorly burnt coal fuses together and forms on the fire grate, restricting the airflow from below.

Connecting rod – The rod running between the crosshead and the coupled wheels (usually but not always the rear-most) transforming the fore-and-aft motion of the pistons into rotary motion on the wheels.

Coupled, or driving wheels – The main wheels of a locomotive that transmit the propulsion created by the cylinders to the rails.

Coupling rod – The rod connecting the coupled wheels together allowing propulsive motion from the cylinders to be transmitted to them all.

Crank – A pear-shaped metal plate on a coupled wheel or a block mounted on its axle, its other end housing the pin for the coupling and/or connecting rod.

ABOVE Departure on the Welshpool & Llanfair Light Railway – the loco has its drain cocks open.

Crank pins – Steel pins mounted on the coupled wheels or cranks, on to which are fitted the connecting and coupling rods.

Crosshead – A commonly H-shaped plate running between bars on the cylinder, on which is mounted the piston rod and the leading end of the connecting rod.

Crown – The top of the inner firebox, below which the water level must never fall while a fire is lit.

Cylinder – A sealed tube into which steam is admitted at either end, pushing a piston to create a fore-and-aft movement to drive the wheels.

Damper – Doors mounted in the ash pan, controlled from the cab and used to regulate the amount of primary air passing to the fire above.

Dart – A flat-ended rod in the centre of a smokebox door which is used to close and lock it.

Dead centre – The point where the piston changes direction in the cylinder.

Displacement lubricator – A type of lubricator in which steam is condensed into hot water, emulsifying with the oil and passing it into the cylinders to lubricate them. See also *Hydrostatic lubricator.*

Dome – The raised section at the top of the boiler used to collect the driest, most efficient steam for passing to the cylinders. A popular location for the regulator valve.

Drain cock – Taps located at the base of cylinders, controlled from the cab and through which steam is passed to eject water that has collected in the cylinders while the locomotive has been standing.

Eccentric – A crank fitted to the driving axle to create motion to drive the valves.

Ejector – A cab-operated device that uses steam to expel air from the train brake pipes enabling a vacuum brake system to work.

Expansion link – An essential component of Stephenson Link motion, which changes the geometry of the motion to control the pace and direction of the locomotive.

Fairlie – A form of articulated locomotive in which one (the single Fairlie) or two (the double Fairlie) power bogies are mounted under a frame on which the boiler and cab are carried. The double Fairlie has two boilers with one firebox between them.

Feed pump – An early means of admitting water to the boiler, driven from an axle. Superseded by the injector.

Firebar – Cast iron bars placed individually into a firebox to form a grate on which the fire is laid.

Firebox – A sandwich-constructed box structure with the firehole door at the rear and the boiler barrel to the front. The inner firebox sits within the outer firebox, with the fire in the inner firebox heating water held between the two boxes.

Fitted/unfitted – Fitted trains have all vehicles joined by a continuous braking system controlled from the locomotive and the guard's compartment. Unfitted trains, usually freight, have individually controlled brakes on each vehicle.

Flue – Boiler tubes of larger diameter fitted in the upper section of the boiler, with superheater elements within them.

Foundation ring – A square or rectangular section ring of metal fitted at the base of the firebox which connects the inner and outer fireboxes together.

Frame – Part of the 'chassis' of the locomotive, which can be of flat plate or bar construction. See also *Running gear*

Fusible plug – These are fitted in the crown (top) of the firebox and are similar to washout plugs, but with a hole through their centre filled with lead. If the temperature becomes too hot, usually due to too low a water level, the lead melts (known as 'dropping a plug'), allowing water into the firebox and alerting the crew to the issue.

Garratt – A form of articulated locomotive with two power bogies mounted under fore and aft fuel tenders, with the boiler and cab slung between them.

Gauge – The distance between the insides of rails. The most widely used 'Standard' gauge is 4ft 8½in (1,435mm). 'Broad' gauge is anything wider, but generally refers to former GWR 7ft 0¼in (2,140mm). 'Narrow' gauge is anything less than standard, but generally refers to 4ft gauge (1,200mm) and under. 'Miniature' is generally regarded as under 15in (450mm).

Gauge glass – A tubular glass mounted in the cab, vertically or close to vertical, showing the amount of water in the boiler. Most locomotives are fitted with two.

Gland – The packing between rods and spindles which is designed to be steam tight.

Gibson ring – A means of securing a steel tyre to a locomotive wheel.

Hopper ash pan – A form of ash pan with a floor that can be tipped to the vertical by a lever action, emptying the ash pan in a single action.

Horns/Horn blocks – Horseshoe-shaped items mounted over the cut outs in the main frames in which the axleboxes move up and down, regulated by the springs.

Horseshoe – A form of fire, thicker at the back and sides of the firebox.

Hydrostatic/Sight feed lubricator – A development of the displacement lubricator, with a glass window allowing monitoring of its use.

Injector – A cab-operated device that uses steam to force water into the boiler under pressure. There are always a minimum of two fitted.

Inside/outside frames – Inside-framed locos have the wheels mounted outside the frames; on outside-framed locos, common on the narrow gauge, the wheels run between the frames.

Irons – Iron bars carried on the footplate to clean the fire with. Typical irons are the pricker, the slice and dart.

Kylchap – A form of blastpipe invented by André Chapelon – superseded by the Lempor type.

Lagging – Heat-resistant matting wrapped around a boiler and held in place by thin steel sheets secured by metal rings known as boiler bands.

Lap – The amount by which a valve covers the steam ports when the piston is at the middle of its stroke.

Lead – The amount of steam that a full stroke of a piston admits into a cylinder.

Lempor – An efficient design of smokebox blastpipe that creates a vacuum in a cylinder as it exhausts steam.

Link and pin – The simplest form of coupling, usually on narrow-gauge stock, in which a vertical pin is used to secure a chain.

Loose/unfitted – A train without a continuous brake, relying on the locomotive and the guard's van to brake it.

Main valve – The fully open position of a regulator.

Mallet – A form of articulated locomotive consisting of a fixed coupled chassis and a power bogie mounted ahead of it.

Mechanical lubricator – A lubrication device directly driven by the locomotive's *motion*.

Meyer – A form of articulated locomotive using two power bogies mounted under a frame which carries the boiler.

MIC – Mutual Improvement Class – traditional steam-age classes for increasing the knowledge of footplate crew. Some heritage lines run MICs today.

Mid-gear – The fully closed position of the reverser.

Motion – The system of rods, cranks and the like used to transmit the fore-and-aft motion produced by a piston into the rotary movement of a wheel, and to drive the valves to maintain the motion. Often incorrectly called 'valve gear' – this is only part of the *motion*.

Mudhole door – Large, removable plates fitted to the firebox and in some cases the boiler barrel to facilitate internal inspections and washouts.

Notch – notch up – A single increment or tooth on the drive of a Reversing lever/Reverser, equivalent to the gearbox of a car. To 'notch up' is to move the reverser closer to its mid-point as speed increases to make the best use of the power available, just as one changes up a gear ratio in a car.

Pannier tank – A form of water storage in which tanks are hung from either side of the boiler, like panniers on a pony.

Pilot valve – The initial open setting of a regulator. Also known as 'first valve'. See also *Main valve*.

Piston/piston rod – A circular plate that is forced by the action of steam upon it to move back and forth inside a cylinder. The piston rod connects the piston to the crosshead.

Piston ring – Metal rings fitted around the edge of a piston to maintain a steam-tight seal with the inside wall of the cylinder.

Piston valve – Effectively a miniature version of a cylinder, governing admission and the exhaust of steam into/from the cylinders themselves. This superseded the slide valve.

Poppet valve – Steam-admission control on Caprotti gear, operated by cams in a similar fashion to the internal combustion engine of a car.

Priming – Water entering the dome and cylinders without being converted to steam first. This is usually caused by overfilling the boiler. In its least serious form the excess is ejected through the chimney as jets of dirty black water. In its most serious form it can cause servere damage through the cylinders failing to compress it.

Quartering – The 90-degree difference between the position of the motion on one side of the locomotive compared with the other.

Regulator – A direct means of driving a locomotive – its 'accelerator'. This is usually a lever but it can be a dial.

Reversing lever/Reverser – A notched lever or a wheel in the cab that alters the geometry of the motion. This is effectively the locomotive's gearbox, but it works equally efficiently in reverse as it does forwards.

Rocking grate – A form of fire grate built as a series of plates which can be rocked to the vertical, dropping the remains of the fire into the ash pan by a single lever action.

Running gear – The main frame, wheels, axleboxes and bearings. Sometimes referred to today by the automotive term of 'chassis'.

Saddle tank – A water storage tank that is positioned over the boiler, like a saddle on a horse.

Safety Valve – A valve placed on top of the boiler and designed to open at a certain pressure (known as 'lifting' or 'blowing off'), to relieve steam pressure in the boiler.

Sander – Boxes connected to pipes and designed to drop sand on to the rail just ahead of the coupled wheels, to aid grip in slippery conditions.

Saturated/superheated steam – Saturated steam is passed into the cylinders from the boiler. Superheated steam is passed back through the boiler several times in pipes ('superheater elements') mounted in the flues before being passed to the cylinders, making it drier and more efficient.

Screw coupling – A standard-fit coupling on standard-gauge locomotives, consisting of two buckles which are tightened using a screw between them.

Shunting – Using a locomotive to manoeuvre rolling stock. On heritage railways, this is usually within station limits.

Slide bars – Horizontal bars fitted to the rear of the cylinders, between which the crosshead runs.

Slide valve – Flat, D-shaped plates running in steam chests and controlling admission and exhaust of steam in the cylinders. This was later superseded by the piston valve.

Slipping – When locomotive wheels break traction with the rail head. If not controlled it can cause serious damage.

Smokebox – The vacuum-sealed tube mounted ahead of the boiler, with the front tubeplate of the boiler tube ends forming its rear. Contains the blastpipe, into which the cylinders exhaust, steam and smoke passing through the chimney mounted on top of the smokebox.

Snifting valve – This opens when a locomotive is coasting to prevent ash from the smokebox being drawn into steam chests, due to the vacuum in the cylinders.

SPAD – Signal passed at danger, which results in disciplinary proceedings.

Spark arrestor – Mesh placed over the smokebox blastpipe to catch sparks and prevent lineside fires.

Spectacle plate – The front plate of a cab.

Staff/staff and ticket/token – Metal items used to protect sections of line. The driver may only enter the section of a single-track line if he is in possession of one of these items.

Stays – Steel or copper bolts threaded at either end connecting the inner and outer firebox plates and forming a water space between the two.

Steam brake – A braking system which uses a steam-driven cylinder to operate the brake linkage.

BELOW Saddle tank locos of varying sizes at the Welsh Slate Museum, Llanberis.

Steam chests – Boxes mounted on the cylinders in which either piston or slide valves run, regulating the entry and exhaust of steam into and out of the cylinders.

Stephenson Link motion – An early but very successful form of motion invented by two employees of railway pioneer George Stephenson.

Stretcher – A plate joining main frame members together and running perpendicular to them. The foremost stretcher (and rearmost on a tank engine) form the bufferbeams.

Superheater – A method of further heating steam before admission to the cylinders by passing it back through the boiler in flues. See *Saturated/superheated steam*.

Tender – A wagon permanently attached to the rear of a locomotive for carrying coal (or oil or wood fuel) and water.

Thermic syphon – Large pipes fitted to some later locomotives, passing through the firebox for heating water more effectively.

Top feed – A system invented by GWR Chief Mechanical Engineer G.J. Churchward, with boiler feed clacks on top of the boiler so that water is pre-heated in the pipes running around the boiler.

Tubeplate – The plates fitted at either end of the boiler in which the ends of the boiler tubes are fixed.

Truck – See *Bogie* and *pony trucks.*

Tyres – The outer steel rim, fitted to a wheel, which makes contact with the rail. These can be replaced when worn.

Vacuum brake – A braking system in which each vehicle is connected by flexible pipes and a vacuum is created. Destroying the vacuum by means of a cab control or a leak in the pipes applies the brakes.

Warming plate – A metal plate above the firehole door on which oil cans are placed.

Washout – A regular procedure of forcing high-pressure water through various holes throughout the boiler and firebox to clean out the insides to remove scale and other waste.

Washout plug – Threaded metal plugs placed in various locations throughout the boiler and firebox to facilitate washouts (See above.)

Walschaerts motion – A form of motion invented by Belgian Egide Walschaerts which largely superseded Stephenson Link motion. It is a two-part system which is equally able to be mounted on the outside of, or between, a locomotive's frames.

Well tank – A water storage tank mounted below the boiler, in between the frames.

Westinghouse brake – A development of the air brake invented by American George Westinghouse, with safeguards against failure of the air supply releasing the brakes.

Worsted trimming – This is made of worsted yarn and placed in oil filler boxes to syphon oil into a hole to lubricate components.

Suggested further reading

Locomotive management

Handbook for Railway Steam Locomotive Enginemen, British Transport Commission, 1957. The famed 'black book' reference guide regarded by many as essential reading for aspiring footplate crews. Republished several times, most recently by Ian Allan Publishing, also regularly found on online auction sites such as eBay.

Tornado Owner's Workshop Manual, Haynes Publishing. In-depth study of new-build A1 Pacific locomotive *Tornado*. Useful for identifying the various components described in this book, as applied to a specific mainline locomotive.

The Design, Construction and Working of Locomotive Boilers, Alan J. Haigh, 2003. In-depth technical appraisal of locomotive boilers.

A number of locomotive management and technical description books were published by the old railway companies and technical bodies in the days of steam. While long out of print and not available new today they can often be found second-hand and through online auction sites such as eBay. They are a useful means of increasing locomotive knowledge. Examples include:

The Locomotive its Features and Remedies by Thomas Pearce, first published in 1896.

Locomotive Management – from cleaning to driving published by the St Margaret's Technical Press, first edition in 1908.

The Locomotive of Today published by the Locomotive Publishing Co at the end of the 19th century.

The Handbook for Steam Railway Locomotive Enginemen, a pocket-sized book published by the London Midland & Scottish Railway in the 1940s and consisting entirely of questions and answers on all aspects of locomotives.

The Locomotive Manufacturers Association Handbook published from 1949 and giving very detailed technical descriptions of all aspects of steam locomotives. It has many drawings and even a glossary of components in four languages!

Many heritage railways have detailed technical descriptions of specific locomotives used on their lines, describing for example, where various components are located and their method of operation. The aspiring footplate crew should familiarise themselves with these.

Signalling

Two Centuries of Railway Signalling, G. Kichenside and A. Williams, 1998, Oxford Publishing Company. In-depth description of railway signalling over the years.

How to be a Railway Signalman, Dave Walden, 2014, Ian Allan Publishing. A recent book aimed at those intending to work in signalling on heritage railways, but includes much useful information for footplate crew.

Heritage Railways

Railways Restored, A former annual guide published by Ian Allan Publishing, detailing all UK heritage railways, rolling stock, opening times, driver experience courses etc. (The 34th and last edition published in 2013.)

Magazines

The regular magazines are an excellent way of keeping up to date on the heritage railway scene and footplate opportunities.

The four major magazines are:

Steam Railway, published four-weekly by Bauer Media and covering all aspects of the steam scene. Website: www.steamrailway.co.uk

Heritage Railway, published four-weekly by Mortons Media and covering steam, diesel and electric preservation. Website: www.heritagerailway.co.uk

The Railway Magazine, the UK's oldest railway magazine, published since 1897 covering both current and heritage subjects. Described as 'Britain's best-selling rail title', it is published monthly by Morton's Media. Website: www.railwaymagazine.co.uk

Narrow Gauge World, specialises in narrow-gauge railways, both UK and worldwide. Published nine times a year (monthly in summer, bi-monthly in winter) by Atlantic Publishers. Website: www.atlanticpublishers.com/magazines/narrow-gauge-world/

Useful addresses

Heritage railways

There are many heritage railways across the UK in widely varying environments, and of both standard and narrow gauges. The most practical way to search for a line near you is to look on the website of the Heritage Railway Association, the umbrella body for the UK's preserved railways. As well as including a great deal of information for the railway enthusiast, this site also offers an online list of all UK heritage railways, with links to lines'

own websites which give details of footplate experiences etc. Website: www.heritagerailways.com/Visits_Map.php

For those searching for footplate experiences the first step should be to check the website of a railway one favours, as they carry detailed information on footplate courses. Alternatively, one can access a range of courses by simply putting 'footplate experience' into an online search engine such as Google.

Suppliers of overalls and footplate equipment

Footplate Equipment Ltd
Tel: 01946 724090 (after 7pm).
E-mail: info@footplateequipent.co.uk
Website: www.footplateequipment.co.uk

North Yorkshire Moors Railway
Shed shop   Tel: 01947 895682.
E-mail: shedshop@nymr.co.uk
Website: www.nymr.co.uk/shedshop

Driver experience courses

The UK railways listed below, standard gauge (SG), narrow gauge (NG) or miniature (MIN), run footplate courses, but the list is not necessarily exhaustive and it is always worth enquiring of your nearest heritage line to see if they offer such a service. For prices and availability one

should check the relevant line's website.

Also well known is the 'Footplate Days & Ways Ltd' course. This is six stages of footplate experiences run by former British Railways driver Clive Groome. Details are at www.steamway.dircon.co.uk or on 01903 207 587.

Amberley Museum, Sussex (NG), 01798 831370, www.amberleynarrowgauge.co.uk
Avon Valley Railway, Bristol (SG), 0117 932 5538, www.avonvalleyrailway.org
Bala Lake Railway, Gwynedd (NG), 01678 540666, www.bala-lake-railway.co.uk
Barry Tourist Railway, Glamorgan (SG), 01446 748816, www.barrytouristrailway.co.uk
Battlefield Line, Leicestershire (SG), 01827 880754, www.battlefield-line-railway.co.uk
Bodmin & Wenford Railway, Cornwall (SG), 01208 73555, www.bodminrailway.co.uk
Bo'ness & Kinneil Railway, Scotland (SG), 01506 822298, www.bkrailway.co.uk
Bredgar & Wormshill Light Railway (NG), 01622 884254, www.bwlr.co.uk
Bure Valley Railway, Norfolk (NG), 01263 733858, www.bvrw.co.uk
Chasewater Railway, Staffordshire (SG), 01543 452623, www.chasewaterrailway.co.uk
Chinnor & Princes Risborough Railway, Oxfordshire (SG), 07784 189322, www.chinnorrailway.co.uk
Churnet Valley Railway, Staffordshire (SG), 01538 750755, www.churnet-valley-railway.co.uk

Colne Valley Railway, Essex (SG), 01787 461174, www.colnevalleyrailway.co.uk
Dean Forest Railway, Gloucestershire (SG), 01594 845840, www.deanforestrailway.co.uk
Didcot Railway Centre, Oxfordshire (SG), 01235 817200, www.didcotrailwaycentre.org.uk
East Anglian Railway Museum, Essex (SG), 01206 242524, www.earm.co.uk
East Lancashire Railway, Lancashire (SG), 07814 302 813, www.eastlancsrailway.org.uk
East Somerset Railway, Somerset (SG), 01749 880417, www.eastsomersetrailway.com
Elsecar Heritage Railway, South Yorkshire (SG), 01226 746746, www.elsecarrailway.co.uk
Exbury Steam Railway, Hampshire (MIN), 023 8089 1203, www.exbury.co.uk
Fairbourne Railway, Gwynedd (MIN), 01341 250362, www.fairbournerailway.com
Foxfield Railway, Staffordshire (SG), 01782 396210, www.foxfieldrailway.co.uk
Gloucestershire Warwickshire Railway, Gloucestershire (SG), 01242 621405, www.gwsr.com
Great Central Railway, Leicestershire (SG), 01509 632323, www.gcrailway.co.uk
Gwili Railway, Carmarthen (SG), 01267 238213, www.gwili-railway.co.uk
Isle of Wight Steam Railway (SG), 01983 885924, www.iwsteamrailway.co.uk
Keighley & Worth Valley Railway, West Yorkshire (SG), 01535 645214, www.kwvr.co.uk
Kent & East Sussex Railway, Kent (SG), 01580 765155, www.kesr.org.uk
Kirklees Light Railway, West Yorkshire (NG), 01484 865727, www.kirkleeslightrailway.com
Lakeside & Haverthwaite Railway, Cumbria (SG), 015395 31594, www.lakesiderailway.co.uk
Lavender Line, East Sussex (SG), 01825 750515, www.lavender-line.co.uk
Lincolnshire Wolds Railway, Lincolnshire (SG), www.lincolnshirewoldsrailway.co.uk
Llangollen Railway, Denbighshire (SG), 01978 860979, www.llangollen-railway.co.uk
Lynton & Barnstaple Railway, Devon (NG), 01598 763487, www.lynton-rail.co.uk
Mid-Hants Railway, Hampshire (SG), 01962 733810, www.watercressline.co.uk
Midland Railway-Butterley, Derbyshire (SG), 01773 747674, www.midlandrailway-butterley.co.uk
Nene Valley Railway, Cambridgeshire (SG), 01780 784444, www.nvr.org.uk
North Norfolk Railway, Norfolk (SG), 01263 820800, www.nnrailway.co.uk
North Yorkshire Moors Railway, North Yorkshire (SG), 01751 472508, www.nymr.co.uk
Peak Rail, Derbyshire (SG), 01629 580381, www.peakrail.co.uk
Perrygrove Railway, Gloucestershire (MIN), 01594 834991, www.perrygrove.co.uk
Romney, Hythe & Dymchurch Railway, Kent (NG), 01797 362353, www.rhdr.org.uk
Rudyard Lake Steam Railway, Staffordshire (MIN), 01995 672280, www.rlsr.org
Severn Valley Railway, Shropshire (SG), 01562 757900, www.svr.co.uk
Sittingbourne & Kemsley Light Railway, Kent (NG), 01795 424899, www.sklr.net
South Devon Railway, Devon (SG), 01364 644370, www.southdevonrailway.co.uk
Spa Valley Railway, Kent (SG), 01892 537715, www.spavalleyrailway.co.uk
Strathspey Railway, Scotland (SG), 01479 810 725, www.strathspeyrailway.co.uk
Swanage Railway, Dorset (SG), 01929 475207, www.swanagerailway.co.uk
Swindon & Cricklade Railway, Wiltshire (SG), 01793 771615, www.swindon-cricklade-railway.org
Talyllyn Railway, Gwynedd (NG), 01654 710472, www.talyllyn.co.uk
Telford Steam Railway, Shropshire (SG), 01952 503880, www.telfordsteamrailway.co.uk
Welsh Highland Heritage Railway, Gwynedd (NG), 01766 513402, www.whr.co.uk
Welshpool & Llanfair Light Railway, Powys (NG), 01938 810441, www.wllr.org.uk
West Lancashire Light Railway, Lancs (NG), 01772 815881, www.westlancs.org
West Somerset Railway, Somerset (SG), 01643 704996, www.westsomersetrailway.vticket.co.uk

Index